Contents

Introduction

Welcome to the world of hospitality digital marketing! This is gonna be fun. Digital marketing for hospitality is different from other types of businesses. When someone visits a restaurant for a meal or checks into a hotel, he or she is making an emotional as well as financial investment. It's not like getting an oil change or buying groceries. Your customers come to you to escape. Your customers come to be entertained – to have a good time. As such, you can't just rely on traditional SEO, paid ads and the like. We are going to discuss those tools because you need to understand them and they need to be part of your digital marketing plan. But you will use these tools in the context of a strategy that is very particular to hospitality.

You have to be an entertainer...a news anchor...a weatherman.

You have to be a historian...a joke teller...and someone people trust.

Your digital marketing should be an extension of who you are, not just what you sell. It should reflect your values, and showcase what is unique about you.

The good thing is that it can be a lot of fun promoting a hotel or restaurant. The bad part is that it takes a lot of time. And if you do it right...it is tiring. Not just in a mental kind of way, either, but literally physically taxing.

We are not talking about hiring a company halfway across the country that is going to write generic articles and do generic marketing. This is not generic "top ten reasons to do XXX" type of content. If you do that, no matter how interesting or unique your business, online your property will look just like everybody else.

Your marketing must be personal! It must be relevant and timely. It must come from the heart. This is not just "soft" stuff for the sake of being soft. This will give you a real, decided advantage over your competition. Why? Because most businesses are just not going to put in the effort.

I call the type of marketing I am going to describe here as "marketing by walking around."

As a hospitality business, you have a built-in advantage when it comes to telling your story. You know the people in your town. You know the businesses in your town. You know what is going on in your town. And those things that you know are the key to making this strategy work.

If you are in a busy tourist area, this is made easier because there are likely to be more unique places to go and events to attend – more things to talk about. But no matter where you are located, if people are coming to stay overnight in your hotel or to eat in your restaurant, then that gives you the opportunity to be a valuable resource. And that is where your leverage is.

You must think of yourself not merely as a the proprietor of a business. You must think of yourself as a storyteller. A photographer. A movie maker. The absolute expert on everything going on in your town. You have the information your customers need!

Again, this is a different type of marketing than what you may be used to. It is very personal. As I mentioned above, it is also physically taxing (although good for you!). Marketing by walking does in fact involve...walking around. If you want to crush your competition, you've got to lace those sneakers up and get walking (or, you know, hire someone to do the walking for you).

This easy-to-read book first lays out all the basic components of a sound digital marketing campaign that any hotel or restaurant can implement. And then I layer the "marketing by walking around" concept on top of it. That is the fuel that makes this thing come to life.

And just so you know, this is not theoretical stuff. I actually do this. I enjoy the work (although my knees, not so much sometimes). I get out, I walk around town, I breathe some fresh air, I take a ton of photos and videos, and I spend time every day cutting all that material up into snippets of content for social media, blog posts, YouTube and various other things. My clients see fantastic results so I can say with 100% certainty THIS STUFF WORKS.

So let's get into it!

Chapter 1: the Basics

How Hospitality Digital Marketing is Different

Marketing a hospitality business is different from marketing other types of businesses in several ways, including:

- **Target Audience.** Hospitality businesses can have a wide and diverse target audience, including leisure and business travelers, families, and groups. Understanding the specific needs and preferences of each segment is critical to developing effective marketing strategies. Are you targeting business travelers? Groups? Families? Romantic couples? It's probably some of all of them, but where do you make most of your money? What is your most profitable segment?

- **Multichannel Marketing.** You very likely already engage in traditional media marketing of some type. Your digital marketing needs to jive with that. It all needs to be consistent. This requires a comprehensive and integrated marketing approach, with a focus on both digital and traditional marketing methods.

- **Location-Based Marketing.** The location of a hotel or restaurant is a critical factor in its marketing strategy. Location-based marketing strategies, such as using local search and social media, can help you reach potential guests who are nearby and looking for a place to stay or eat.

- **Experience-Driven Marketing.** Hospitality businesses are experience-driven businesses, and the quality of the guest experience is a critical factor in driving sales and loyalty. Your marketing strategies should focus on showcasing the unique aspects of your business and the experiences it offers to potential guests.

- **Seasonal Fluctuations.** Hospitality businesses often experience seasonal fluctuations in demand, which can impact their marketing strategies and tactics. Understanding these fluctuations and adjusting marketing strategies accordingly is crucial to success. However, you should never stop marketing, even during slow times.

Seasonality and Cyclicality

Let's talk a bit more about seasonality and cyclicality because it affects the hospitality sector more than other types of businesses. You likely already know the seasonal aspects of your business. You know the times of year, month, week, day of week, and even time of day when you do the most business.

A review of your website analytics will mirror your real-world experience with regard to seasonality. If you are in a tourist location, you probably do more business during warmer months (or it could be the opposite, such as if you are in a snow skiing location).

If there are already natural cycles that occur in your business, should you even bother marketing during your slower times?

Yes! Maybe even more! When overall business in your town is down, that is when you want to do MORE marketing. That is an opportunity to spread your brand and pick up market share. Many of your competitors are probably putting the brakes on during these times, which is why you want to put on steam.

The exception is when dealing with paid marketing where you need to maximize your return on investment. In that scenario, you need to spend your marketing dollars during their most effective times, which may mean not running ads during slower times. The "marketing by walking around" process creates content that is evergreen – that sticks around – as opposed to paid ads, which go away once you stop paying.

The strategies discussed in this book must be applied year-around. Never stop marketing. When your competitors slow down, you should do even more.

A Primer on Digital Marketing

Digital marketing, at least as we are going to discuss it, is using the Internet to promote your business. That could mean using Google to drive traffic to your website, promoting a Facebook business Page, sending a newsletter to an email list, running mobile phone ads, or any number of similar technologies. But you don't want to do this stuff haphazardly, a little bit of this a little bit of that, in a random fashion. Whatever components go into your campaign, it needs to be well-orchestrated, and everything needs to make sense and fit together. As mentioned above, it also needs to be consistent with whatever offline marketing you currently do.

Promoting your business online has a few advantages over traditional media marketing, like radio and print ads. These include:

- You can get great exposure for your business in search engines and on social media platforms using nothing more than your own hard work and consistency.

- Online ads can be changed instantly. It can take days or weeks to change a traditional print, radio or TV ad. This allows you to adjust ads rapidly based on real time data.

- Online media can be automatically split-tested. Running two ads at once and comparing results can help you improve your ad performance.

- Online marketing budgets can be changed any time. Need to run an ad for one day but only have $5? No problem. You can be on Google this afternoon.

- The digital market continues to grow. Everybody has a smart phone now. Everybody is using his or her phone to search for information. Businesses that take advantage of that will gain a competitive advantage.

- Internet marketing, and social media in particular, creates a communication channel that is much more personal than any kind of traditional media.

- Targeted marketing can put your business in front of people looking for lodging or a place to eat in exactly your market.

There is a lot to like about digital marketing.

Components of a Digital Marketing Campaign

There are five main components to a digital marketing campaign as we are going to discuss it:

1. **Your Website.** Your website is like your own little piece of Internet real estate. It is also

where you will take reservations. It is radically critical that your website be mobile friendly and easy to use, which we will discuss later.

2. **Search Engine Optimization (SEO).** This is the process of optimizing a website so that it appears highly in organic (non-paid) search engine results for specific target keywords. So if you own a hotel in Nashville, Tennessee, you would want your website to appear prominently in Google when someone searches for "Nashville hotel." The things you do to make this happen are called SEO.

   Sidenote: it is actually EXTREMELY difficult to rank an individual hotel for a search like that. The booking aggregators like hotels.com and booking.com dominate those rankings. Where an individual hotel can generally appear is in the local/map section. For that reason, you will want to target a wide basket of keywords – some broad, and some very specific. You also want to engage in "local SEO" to improve your positioning in the local/map rankings. We will discuss this in more detail later.

3. **Paid Search.** This is using one of numerous online advertising platforms such as Google Ads or Bing Ads to drive traffic to your website. It generates a similar result as SEO, with the difference being that you actually pay a certain amount of money for each click. Included in this

general category is the process of running graphical ads on third party (non-search) websites.

4. **Social Media.** Social media platforms like Facebook, Twitter and Instagram can all generate awareness for your business and drive traffic to your website. They also provide the opportunity to have one-on-one conversations with prospective customers. If you're going to use these to promote your business, you've got to be more strategic than just doing personal Facebook updates every now and then. It must be systematic.

5. **Email.** I will make the wild assumption that you know what email is. In terms of Internet marketing, what we are talking about is building a list of email addresses of prospective or past customers to whom you send some kind of regular communication like a newsletter. For hospitality businesses in locations that are popular tourist destinations, this is an especially useful tool because you can keep your list updated on special events happening in the area. Tell them why they should come into town...and then sell them a reservation!

These are high level descriptions that have many sub-components. For example, "SEO" will include local SEO, which is the process of performing SEO specifically for a certain geographic market. A sound Internet marketing strategy makes use of all five of these components to some degree. The one thing missing from the above list is the secret sauce – the "marketing by walking around" part. We'll get into that in a bit.

Now let's discuss each of these five major items in more detail. You probably already know some of this, but I suggest you go ahead and read it all to make sure you are up-to-speed on every component of the campaign we are going to describe.

Note: We are not going to go into great detail about these items. If we were to do that, this would be a thousand-page book that no one would ever read. You need to understand the components of a digital marketing campaign to understand the **marketing by walking around** concept. When it comes to implementing the individual marketing components of the strategy (SEO, social media, email, etc.), there is enough information here to get you started. From there, you can do your own study and experimentation to learn more or hire a professional to take care of it.

Chapter 2: Your website

Obviously, you must have a website. You probably already have one! But I will discuss the factors that will make your website a success.

Domain Name

Your domain name is your address on the web. From an SEO perspective, it can be beneficial to use keywords in the domain. But is it better for your business to have keywords in your domain name, or just to use the name of your business?

Including keywords in your domain name can help your website rank higher in search engine results for those keywords. This can increase visibility and drive more traffic to your site. However, including too many keywords in your domain name can be seen as spammy and negatively impact your search engine ranking.

Using your business name as the domain name can establish your brand and make it easier for customers to remember your website and find it again in the future. However, it may not be optimized for search engines and may not rank as well for relevant keywords.

Ultimately, the best option for your business will depend on your individual marketing goals and target audience. If search engine optimization (SEO) is a high priority, incorporating relevant keywords in your domain name can be beneficial. If the name of your business happens to align with your market (i.e., the name of your hotel is Dallas Inn) then that is the best of both worlds.

Purchasing Another Business's Domain Name

If another business already has a domain name that you want, it is possible to make an offer to purchase. However, there are a few things to keep in mind before making the investment:

- **Availability.** It's possible that the domain name you want is not for sale or that the owner is not interested in selling it. You can use domain name marketplace websites such as GoDaddy Auctions or Sedo to search for available domain names.

- **Cost.** Buying a domain name can be expensive (sometimes REALLY expensive!), especially if it's a popular or in-demand name. Be sure to research the current market value of the domain name you're interested in and determine if the cost is worth it for your business.

- **Legal Considerations.** If the domain name you're interested in is already in use, it's important to ensure that you have the legal right to use it. In some cases, the domain name may be trademarked or copyrighted, and using it without permission could result in legal action.

- **Alternatives.** If the domain name you want is not available or too expensive, consider using alternative domain extensions, such as .net or .biz, or using a modified version of the name that is still recognizable and memorable to your target audience.

Alternative Domain Extensions (gTLD Domains)

It used to be that you were better off with a good ol' .com domain. But those days are over, and it may now even more advantageous to go with one of the MANY available alternative domains (or gTLD domains, which stands for "generic top-level domain"). Here are a few examples of interesting gTLD domains that could be useful for a hospitality business:

- .beer

- .best

- .boutique

- .coffee

- .farm

- .kitchen

- .pizza

- .restaurant

- .villas

To see a much longer list of these options, visit **www.godaddy.com/domains/gtld-domain-names**.

Example: You own a pizza restaurant in Des Moines. You could use the domain name desmoines.pizza. It clearly describes what your restaurant is and it will help with search visibility. Not bad!

The downside is that these domains tend to be more expensive, often starting around $75 per year, and sometimes way more expensive than that. So don't forget that that is a fee you need to pay every year, or after however many years you purchase the domain for.

Ultimately, buying a domain name is a personal decision that depends on your individual marketing goals and budget. Before making a purchase, be sure to carefully consider the availability, cost, legal considerations, and alternatives to ensure that you're making the best choice for your business.

Hosting

Hosting is the service that makes your website available on the Internet. The files that make up your website live on a server (a computer that "serves" files when requested) that sends your website data to a user's browser when he types your Web address. You need good hosting for your site, so this is not an area to skimp.

When choosing a website hosting provider for your website, there are several factors to consider:

- **Reliability.** Your website hosting provider should offer high uptime and quick load times to ensure that your website is always accessible to potential customers.

- **Security.** Ensure that your hosting provider offers robust security measures, such as SSL encryption, to protect your website and your guests' information. Installing SSL certificates is a pain, so if your hosting company does it for you automatically, that is a huge benefit.

- **Scalability.** As your marketing campaign achieves success, your website traffic will also increase. Choose a hosting provider that can accommodate this growth and provide the necessary resources to keep your website running smoothly. If you have to upgrade your hosting to account for more traffic, that is a good thing! It means your digital marketing is working.

- **Customer Support.** Good customer support is essential in case you encounter any technical issues with your website (and you very likely will at some point). Look for a hosting provider that offers 24/7 support and has a proven track record of resolving problems quickly. I can attest from personal experience that having a hosting company with poor support can make you wanna pull your hair out, so this is very important.

- **Price.** Price is an important consideration, but it should not be the only factor. It's important to balance cost with the other factors mentioned above to ensure that you're getting the best value for your money. Again: don't be cheap! With hosting (as most things in life) you get what you pay for.

Some popular website hosting options include shared hosting, VPS (Virtual Private Server) hosting, and dedicated server hosting. The best choice for your business will depend on the size of your website, the amount of traffic you receive, and your budget.

If you are unsure, consider consulting with a web development professional to determine the best hosting solution for your specific needs. If you take my advice regarding your website, using the WordPress platform, I have specific hosting suggestions later.

Design

Design is an important aspect of a hospitality website, as it can impact the user experience, affect your online visibility, and drive business.

Here are some critical design considerations for your website:

- **User-Friendly Navigation.** The website should be easy to navigate, with clear categories and a simple menu structure, so that users can find the information they need quickly and easily. One menu style I have been using some lately is called a "mega menu." These are large expandable menus that provide much more information than a standard menu, and they break down nicely for mobile screens. These menus are generally launched by clicking an icon (often called a "hamburger," for some reason) that will appear in the corner of the header. You have undoubtedly seen these when viewing websites on your phone.

- **High-Quality Images and Video.** High-quality images and video of your business (rooms and amenities for a hotel, menu items for a restaurant), and local attractions, can help potential guests get a better understanding of what you have to offer. This is where a nice camera can really come in handy. For this type of content, you want maximum professionality. If you use your phone, do your very best to get high quality photos and stage everything to look nice. For example, if you are photographing a meal, make sure the table is nicely set. For that type of photo, I also like to focus on the items in the foreground, with a nice, pleasing blur in the background.

- **Mobile Responsiveness.** With the majority of users accessing websites on mobile devices, it's important that the website is optimized for mobile viewing, with a responsive design that adapts to different screen sizes and devices. You must test your design on different size screens and on different devices.

- **Booking Engine Integration.** A hotel website should include a booking engine that allows users to book rooms directly from the website. This can improve conversion rates and make the booking process more convenient for users. If you restaurant takes reservations, you should implement a method to take reservations on your website.

- **Clear Calls-to-Action.** The website should include clear calls-to-action, such as "Book Now" buttons and forms, that encourage users to take action and make a reservation. Make it very, very, very easy for the website visitor to know what to do.

- **Brand Consistency.** The website should be consistent with your business' brand, using the same colors, fonts, and images as other marketing materials, to reinforce your brand identity and messaging. Leave no doubt in your visitors mind what they are looking at.

- **Fast Load Speed.** The website should load quickly, as users are likely to abandon slow-loading sites. Optimizing images, compressing files, and reducing the number of page elements are some of the basic ways to help improve load speed. As we will discuss later, however, there is much more to it than just the entire site loading quickly. How soon the visitor can begin interacting with the website, even if parts of it are still loading, is very important.

- **Accessible Design.** The website should be accessible to users with disabilities, including those with visual, auditory, or motor impairments. This can include using clear, easy-to-read text, high-contrast color schemes, and alternative text descriptions for images. Two websites you can use to check your website for accessibility are accessibilitychecker.org and pagespeed.web.dev. This goes beyond just being good practice – it can keep you out of legal trouble!

- **User Reviews and Testimonials.** Including user reviews and testimonials on the website can help build trust and credibility with potential guests. This can also provide valuable insights into the guest experience and help inform future marketing and customer service efforts. If people are complaining about your business, you need to fix what they are complaining about!

- **Integration with Social Media.** Your website should include links to your social media profiles and encourage users to follow and engage with your business on social media. This can help build a community of loyal fans and followers and drive social media engagement.

- **Contact Information.** The website should prominently display your contact information, including phone number, email address, and physical address, to make it easy for users to get in touch with you and find you when they are driving around your town. In addition to a separate page with the information, place it in the footer so that it is on every page. This will also encourage Google to show your business in Google Maps.

- **Personalization.** The website can be personalized to each user, based on their interests, location, and previous interactions with your business. This can improve the user experience and increase the likelihood of traffic and reservations.

By incorporating these design considerations into your website, you can create an engaging and user-friendly experience that drives bookings and builds brand awareness.

Website Load Speed

You website must be fast. Later we talk about some of the specific metrics that Google uses to measure your website. But first, here are some tips for making your website load faster:

- **Optimize Images.** Large, high-resolution images can significantly slow down a website's load speed. Use image compression tools to reduce file sizes without sacrificing quality. I do my image work in Photoshop, so that is where I do image compression, but there are also third-party tools that will do it. Compressjpeg.com is one such option. However, you are going to be dealing with a LOT of images, so it is recommended that you purchase some type of image editing software.

- **Minimize HTTP Requests.** The number of HTTP requests a website makes can impact its load speed. Minimizing the number of requests by combining and minifying CSS and JavaScript files, and using CSS sprites, can help reduce load time. This is fairly technical stuff, so you may need some help. If you use WordPress, you can install a plugin that will do this for you.

- **Use a Content Delivery Network (CDN).** A CDN can distribute your website's content across multiple servers, reducing the load on a single server and improving website load speed. If you use a high quality website hosting account, it will likely have a CDN option you can take advantage of.

- **Enable Browser Caching.** Enabling browser caching can allow users' browsers to store frequently-used files locally, reducing the number of files that need to be downloaded with each page load. Be careful with caching that it doesn't prevent new content from being seen by visitors to your site. After posting new content, you may need to clear the cache. After posting new content, always view it in a different browser without being logged in so you know other people can see it as well.

- **Choose a Fast Hosting Provider.** Choosing a fast, reliable hosting provider can make a significant difference in website load speed. Consider hosting options such as cloud hosting, VPS hosting, or dedicated hosting, depending on the size and needs of your website. For WordPress, use dedicated WordPress hosting. I use WPEngine for most of my clients' sites.

By following these tips, you can improve your website's load speed and provide a better user experience for your visitors, which can lead to increased engagement and bookings, as well as improved search rankings.

Website Accessibility

Website accessibility in the hospitality industry, as in any other, is not just about ticking off a box in a compliance checklist. It is about opening up your business to a wider market and offering an equitable online experience to all users, regardless of their physical or cognitive abilities.

Ignoring it will also cost you money!

With a surge in online reservations and digital concierge services, the need for accessible websites is more pressing than ever in the hospitality industry.

Web accessibility refers to the inclusive practice of removing barriers that prevent interaction with, or access to websites, by people with disabilities. When sites are correctly designed, developed, and edited, all users can have equal access to information and functionality. This includes aspects such as providing captions for video content, designing websites to be navigable by keyboard-only input, and coding websites so screen reader software can interpret content for visually impaired users.

Web Content Accessibility Guidelines (WCAG) is a widely-accepted standard for web accessibility. Developed through the W3C process, these guidelines offer a thorough definition of web accessibility and provide specific recommendations for making websites more accessible. They break accessibility down into four key principles: perceivable, operable, understandable, and robust (POUR).

If you want to dig much deeper, check out
www.w3.org/standards/webdesign/accessibility.

Why is Web Accessibility Important?

There are three main reasons why web accessibility is
crucial for the hospitality industry:

- **Business Case.** Approximately 15% of the
world's population experience some form of
disability. Ensuring your website is accessible
allows you to tap into a significant demographic
that is often overlooked. Furthermore, even
those without disabilities can benefit from
accessible design, known as the curb-cut effect.
For example, subtitles are helpful for those with
hearing impairments but can also aid users in a
loud environment or those who prefer reading
content. In other words, it's good business and
can be a competitive advantage.

- **Legal Requirements.** Around the world,
legislation such as the Americans with
Disabilities Act (ADA) and the UK Equality Act
mandates businesses to make their websites
accessible to people with disabilities. Failure to
comply with these laws can result in lawsuits
and fines, damage to your brand's reputation,
and lost business opportunities.

- **Ethical Obligation.** Providing equal access to
services and information is a fundamental

human right outlined in the United Nations Convention on the Rights of Persons with Disabilities. Businesses have an ethical duty to ensure their websites are accessible to everyone.

How to Test for Website Accessibility

Testing for website accessibility can be carried out in various ways:

- **Automated Accessibility Checkers.** Tools such as Google's Lighthouse, WebAIM's WAVE, or the Accessibility Insights for Web extension can provide a fast overview of potential accessibility issues.

- **Manual Testing.** This involves using a website as a person with a disability might, using only keyboard navigation, or using screen reading software.

- **Professional Accessibility Audit.** Engaging an accessibility expert to perform an in-depth review can provide the most comprehensive insight into how accessible your website is and where improvements can be made.

Making Your Site Accessible and Compliant

Use Accessible Design Principles. Follow the principles of accessible design. Make sure that all images have alt text. Use headings correctly to structure your content. Make sure your site works well with screen readers.

Do the things we talk about in the sections in this book about website design and on-page optimization and most of it will be done. Also do the following:

- **Create Inclusive Content.** This means captions for videos, transcripts for audio content, and descriptive text for images.

- **Follow WCAG Guidelines.** The WCAG 2.1 guidelines are a thorough resource for making your website more accessible. They offer recommendations such as offering text alternatives for non-text content and providing ways for users to navigate and find content.

- **Regularly Test Your Website.** Regular testing ensures your site remains accessible even as it is updated and changed. Use the services listed earlier.

Website accessibility is a necessity in the modern digital landscape, particularly in the hospitality industry. It's not just about compliance—it's a vital part of providing an excellent customer experience and ensuring your services are available to the broadest possible audience.

Booking Engine

When choosing a booking engine for a hotel website, it's important to consider the following factors:

- **User Experience.** The booking engine should be easy to use and provide a seamless experience for guests. It should be intuitive, with clear calls-to-action and options for choosing dates, room types, and other preferences. The LAST thing you want to do is make it hard for your visitors to figure out how to make a reservation!

- **Mobile Optimization.** With increasing numbers of users accessing the internet on mobile devices, it's important that the booking engine is optimized for mobile devices. This includes ensuring that the booking process is fast, responsive, and easy to complete on a mobile device. Test it out yourself on your own phone as well as other devices.

- **Integration with PMS.** The booking engine should integrate seamlessly with the hotel's property management system (PMS) to ensure that real-time room availability is displayed to guests and that bookings are reflected in the PMS in real-time. Without that integration, you will end up double-booking rooms, which creates a bad situation for you to have to deal with.

- **Payment Processing.** The booking engine should securely process payments and support a range of payment options, including credit and debit cards, PayPal, and other payment methods.

- **Customization.** The booking engine should offer options for customization, including the ability to add the hotel's brand and colors, to display custom content and promotions, and to set up up-sell and cross-sell offers.

- **Reporting and Analytics.** The booking engine should provide reporting and analytics capabilities to help the hotel better understand its booking trends and make data-driven decisions about its marketing and pricing strategies. Make sure your booking engine can provide revenue data to your analytics! At the end of the day, that is the most important metric. You want to be able to see exactly where your sales are coming from.

- **Support and Service.** The booking engine provider should offer responsive and knowledgeable customer support and regular software updates to ensure that the booking engine remains up-to-date and secure.

You must have a good booking engine for your website. For a hotel, being able to take a reservation is the most important part!

Copy

Good copywriting can be a key factor in helping your website attract and convert visitors into customers. Here are some tips for writing effective copy for your website:

- **Know Your Target Audience.** Understand who your target audience is and what their needs, interests, and pain points are. Tailor your copy to speak directly to them and address their specific needs and concerns. Are your customers in town on business? Are they tourists? Are they mostly locals? Are they in a hurry, or can they take their time?

- **Highlight Unique Features and Benefits.** What sets your hotel or restaurant apart from others? Highlight the unique features and benefits that make you a standout choice for guests.

- **Use Clear and Concise Language.** Write in a conversational tone and use clear, concise language that is easy to understand. Don't try to be overly sophisticated unless that style of language suits your audience.

- **Optimize for Search Engines.** Use keywords and phrases that are relevant to your business and target audience, and that are likely to be used by guests when searching for a hotel or restaurant online. This will help improve your website's search engine ranking and visibility. More about this below.

- **Showcase Visual Content.** Use high-quality images and videos to showcase your hotel's rooms and facilities. A restaurant should showcase beautiful photos of your food and restaurant interior. Show photos of your exterior and from around town. This will help to bring your copy to life and give potential guests a better sense of what they can expect when they do business with you.

- **Tell a Story.** People respond to stories, so consider incorporating storytelling elements into your copy. This can help to build a connection with your audience and make your business feel more approachable and relatable. If there is a historic element to your business, tell that history. If there's not much history to the business, tell YOUR history! Businesses don't just appear from thin air. Somebody had a dream, and he or she turned that dream into reality. Talk about it.

- **Call to Action.** Make sure your copy includes clear calls-to-action that encourage visitors to take action, such as booking a room, making a reservation, requesting more information, or signing up for your email list.

The above actions will help you write copy for your website that engages and converts visitors into customers. Don't skimp on this process. Put some real time into it. Your website can a 24/7 sales machine for your business if it has well-written, compelling copy.

Chapter 3: Search Engine Optimization

Search Engine Optimization, "SEO", is doing certain things that will encourage Google and other search engines to rank your website highly in searches for specific keywords. It increases traffic to your website from people who are looking for information about your type of business.

Here are the basic things you need to do to optimize your website:

- Optimize the website's content and structure for relevant keywords and phrases that potential guests may use when searching for a hotel or restaurant.

- Build backlinks to the website from other reputable websites to improve its authority and search engine rankings.

- Create and optimize local listings and profiles on directories such as Google My Business, Yelp and TripAdvisor to improve visibility in local search results.

- Create unique and engaging content such as blog posts, videos, and customer reviews to attract and engage potential guests.

- Optimize the website code, images and videos to improve the website's loading speed, which can have a positive impact on search engine rankings.

- Using analytics and tracking tools to monitor the website's performance and make data-driven decisions to improve its SEO.

Keyword Research

Keywords are the words that people use to search the Web for a particular type of business or service. These words should be used strategically on your website to capture as much of that traffic as possible. A mistake that many business owners make is that they THINK they know what those words are, but they really don't.

Don't guess about what search terms someone might use to search for lodging or food in your area. Perform a process called keyword research to find out for sure what those words are. Google provides its own keyword research tool that will give you solid data to tell you what keywords you should be targeting.

You should use a mix of keywords for SEO, including:

- **Location-based Keywords.** These include the name of the city, state, or region where your business is located, as well as any landmark or attraction that is near you. For example, "New York City hotel," "Chicago downtown hotel," "San Francisco Union Square hotel," "Nashville restaurant," "Atlanta barbecue," etc.

- **Room and Rate-related Keywords.** These include terms related to the type of room or rate that a guest might be searching for. For example, "Budget hotel," "Luxury hotel," "Family hotel," "Suites hotel," "Discount hotel," etc. For a restaurant, it could be keywords like "fine dining" and "family restaurant."

- **Amenity-related Keywords.** These include terms related to the amenities and services that the hotel offers. For example, "Free wifi," "Pool," "Fitness center," "Restaurant," "Bar," etc.

- **Review-related Keywords.** These include terms related to the quality of service and guest reviews. For example, "Best hotel," "Top-rated hotel," "5-star hotel," "best pizza," "award-winning," etc.

It's important to note that you should always consider the intent of the user who is searching for keywords, so you can make sure you are targeting the right audience.

There are several ways to find the best SEO keywords for your website:

- **Conduct Keyword Research.** Use keyword research tools such as Google Keyword Planner, Ahrefs, SEMrush, etc. to find out the search volume and competition for different keywords related to hotels or restaurants in your area. These tools can also provide suggestions for related keywords that you may not have thought of.

- **Analyze Your Competitors.** Look at the websites of other hotels or restaurants in your area with strong search visibility and take note of the keywords they are using in their content and meta tags. This will give you an idea of what keywords are working for them and can provide inspiration for your own website.

- **Use Google Autocomplete.** Type a phrase related to your business into Google's search bar and pay attention to the suggestions that come up. These are often popular search queries that people use when looking for your type of business.

- **Analyze Your Data.** Use your own Google Analytics, Google Search Console data or other analytics tools to find out which keywords are currently driving traffic to your website. You can also see which pages on your website are performing well and which ones are not, this will give you an idea of what to optimize. We will discuss Google Search Console in more detail later.

- **Ask Your Customers.** Ask your guests how they found you or what words they used when searching for a hotel or dining. This will give you insight into the keywords that are resonating with your target audience.

Using Google Keyword Planner

Google Keyword Planner is a free tool designed for advertisers but also serves as an excellent resource for SEO keyword research. It is where I recommend you begin your keyword research because it gives you search data straight from the source – Google! It provides insights into keyword ideas, search volume data, competition levels, and bid estimates, enabling you to make informed decisions about the keywords you choose for your website.

Tip: if there are keywords relevant to your business that competitors are paying good money for, chances are good those are high quality, high converting keywords.

Start by brainstorming a list of seed keywords related to your hospitality business. These should include generic terms such as "hotels" and "restaurants." Additionally, think about location-specific keywords like "hotels in [city name]" or "fine dining restaurants near [location]." You will feed these keywords into Keyword Planner tool to get data on those keywords as well as additional keywords that Google will provide.

To use Keyword Planner, go to **ads.google.com/intl/en_us/home/tools/keyword-planner/** Ads (or just go to **ads.google.com**). You will have to create a Google Ads account if you don't already have one.

Google Keyword Planner offers various features to discover keyword ideas:

- **Keyword Planner's Discover New Keywords.** Enter your seed keywords into the "Discover new keywords" section. It will generate additional keyword ideas based on search volume, competition, and relevance. Filter the results based on location and language to ensure local targeting.

- **Competitor Analysis.** Enter your competitors' websites into the "Start with a website" text field to discover keywords they are targeting. Analyzing their strategy can help you uncover valuable keyword opportunities.

- **Search Terms.** If you have been running ads, you can see the performance of the search terms that triggered your ad. This will tell you exactly what terms work the best. We will discuss paid search later, but for now just understand that search terms are different than the keywords you set up in your account.

As you accumulate a list of potential keywords, it's essential to refine and expand it in the following ways:

- **Relevance and Intent.** Assess the relevance and intent behind each keyword. Consider the searchers' motives and align your keywords accordingly. For example, "luxury hotels in [city name]" might be more relevant for high-end establishments.

- **Search Volume and Competition.** Analyze the search volume and competition level for each keyword. Focus on keywords with a good balance between search volume and competition, as overly competitive terms may be harder to rank for.

- **Long-Tail Keywords.** Incorporate long-tail keywords (more specific, multi-word phrases) into your list. They often have lower competition and higher conversion rates, making them valuable for niche targeting. For example, "family-friendly hotels with pool in [city name]" or "[city name] Italian restaurant."

- **Local Keywords.** Emphasize location-specific keywords if your hospitality business relies heavily on local clientele. Optimize for keywords like "best hotels in [city name]" or "top-rated restaurants near [location]."

It can be helpful to group your keywords into themes or categories based on their relevance. This will help you create focused website content and optimize individual pages accordingly. Organizing your keywords also facilitates tracking the performance of each category and adjusting your strategy if needed.

Once you have a list of keywords, you should prioritize them based on their relevance, search volume, and competition. Start by targeting the most relevant and low-competition keywords, then move on to more competitive keywords as your website's search engine rankings improve.

By conducting thorough keyword research, you can ensure that your website is optimized for the keywords that are most relevant to your target audience and that will help you reach your marketing goals. Once you have a basket of keywords to work with, the next step is to USE those keywords on your website in a process called on-page optimization.

On-Page Optimization

Once these keywords are identified, they should be incorporated into the your website copy, page titles, and meta descriptions.

Page titles and meta descriptions are important on-page optimization elements that can have a significant impact on your search engine rankings. Page titles should accurately describe the content of the page and include relevant keywords. They should also be concise and ideally, be under 70 characters to ensure they are fully displayed in search engine results pages ("SERPs").

For example, if a hotel in Miami has a page that lists its amenities, a good page title might be "Luxury Downtown Miami Hotel Amenities – [Hotel Name]." This title incorporates the relevant keywords "hotel amenities" and "Downtown Miami," and it accurately describes the content of the page.

Meta descriptions, on the other hand, provide a brief summary of the page content and are usually displayed in SERPs below the page title. They should be well-written, informative, and include relevant keywords.

For example, a meta description for our hypothetical amenities page might be "Experience the finest amenities at our luxury hotel in downtown Miami. Enjoy breathtaking views, fine dining, and top-notch service during your stay in Miami."

Use Header Tags

Header tags (H1, H2, H3, etc.) help organize content on a webpage and make it easier for users to navigate. They also help search engines understand the structure and hierarchy of the content on the page.

The H1 tag should be used for the main heading of the page and should include relevant keywords.

Subheadings (H2, H3, etc.) can be used to break up the content and should also include relevant keywords.

For example, on a restaurant homepage, the H1 tag might be "Best Barbecue Joint in Nashville, Tennessee" and the H2 subheading something like "The Best Pulled Pork, Ribs and Brisket in Nashville."

Optimize Website Copy

Website copy is one of the most important on-page optimization elements. It should be well-written, informative, and easy to read. It should also incorporate relevant keywords without being over-optimized or spammy.

When optimizing website copy, it's important to focus on creating valuable content that provides information that travelers or diners are looking for. This will include information about amenities, location, menu, nearby attractions, and things to do in the area.

For example, a hotel's homepage copy might read:

"Welcome to our luxury hotel in the heart of Memphis, Tennessee. Our hotel offers guests the best in luxury accommodations, with breathtaking views, world-class dining, and top-notch service. Our central location makes it easy to explore all that the city has to offer, from famous landmarks like the Pyramid, to the vibrant nightlife of Beale Street."

It's also important to include calls-to-action (CTAs) throughout the website copy to encourage users to book a room, make a reservation or visit your location. CTAs should be clear and prominent, and they should direct users to a specific page where they can take action.

For example, a CTA on the homepage might read, "Book your stay today and experience the best in luxury accommodations in St. Louis."

Optimize Site Structure

The structure of your website can also impact its search engine rankings. A well-structured website is easy to navigate and helps users find the information they need quickly and efficiently. It also helps search engines understand the content and hierarchy of the website.

The website should be organized into a clear and logical hierarchy of pages, with the homepage at the top and subpages organized beneath it. Each page should have a unique and descriptive URL that includes relevant keywords.

For example, a page URL for a hotel amenities page might be "www.hotelname.com/amenities." This URL includes relevant keywords and accurately describes the content of the page.

Note: Make sure you don't have page URLs that look like this: *yoursite.com/?p=12* That looks terrible! It provides no clue to search engines or human visitors what the page is about.

In addition, the website should include a sitemap that lists all the pages on the site. This helps search engines crawl and index the site more easily, and it also helps users find the information they need. Speaking of sitemaps, you should also have an XML sitemap. We go into that in more detail in the section about Google Search Console.

Use Alt Text for Images

To optimize images for search engines, you should use descriptive file names and alt text.

Alt text is a brief description of the image that appears when the image cannot be displayed. It helps search engines understand the content of the image and can also improve accessibility for visually impaired users.

For example, if your website features a photo of a steak, you would want it to have alt text like "Bacon-wrapped 7 oz. filet mignon." It feeds Google some nice keywords AND provides an accurate description for accessibility purposes.

Ensure Mobile Responsiveness

In today's mobile-first world, having a mobile-responsive website is essential. A mobile-responsive website is one that adjusts to the size of the user's screen, making it easy to navigate and read on a mobile device.

Having a mobile-responsive website not only improves the user experience but also impacts search engine rankings. Google now considers mobile-friendliness a TOP ranking factor, meaning that sites that are not mobile-responsive will not rank as highly in search results.

To ensure mobile responsiveness, you should use responsive design techniques when building your website. This might include using a flexible grid system, optimizing images for smaller screens, and using responsive navigation menus. If you use a modern WordPress theme, it should handle responsiveness for you, but you need to test everything.

Google Core Web Vitals

We're kind-of getting into some heavy stuff here, but this is very important to understand because it can make a huge difference on your website's performance. "Core Web Vitals" is a term coined by Google to represent a number of items that it analyzes when gauging your website. The idea is that how fast your website loads is not the only important thing – it's how fast the visitor to your website can begin interacting with it. It is based on research done by Google over the years about what provides the best user experience.

Google makes the following claims[1]:

- When a site passes Core Web Vitals, users are 24% less likely to abandon the page while it is loading.

- Reducing Cumulative Layout Shift (CLS) by 0.2 can lead to a 15% increase in page views per session.

- Reducing Cumulate Layout Shift improves domain rankings.

So Just What are the Core Web Vitals?

There are five major metrics that represent Google Core Web Vitals:

---

[1] https://support.google.com/webmasters/answer/9205520

- **First Contentful Paint** – the time at which the first text or image is painted to the screen.

- **Largest Contentful Paint** – the time at which the largest text or image is painted.

- **Total Blocking Time** – the sum of all time periods between First Contentful Paint and when the site becomes interactive.

- **Cumulative Layout Shift** – the movement of visible elements within the screen as the site loads.

- **Speed Index** – how quickly the contents of a page are visibly populated.

In a nutshell, yes, Google wants the page to load quickly, but it also wants people to be able to interact with the page even if it is not loaded completely.

How to Know Your Core Vitals Numbers

To get your Core Web Vitals numbers, visit **pagespeed.web.dev**. Then type in your website address and click Analyze. Google will provide all this information.

In addition to the Core Web Vitals numbers, Google will score your site in four major categories:

- **Performance** – how fast the site loads and is usable. This is the Core Web Vitals stuff.

- **Accessibility** – how usable your site is to those with disabilities. This includes things like the use of image alt tags and high contract between text and background colors. Refer to the section above on Accessibility for more detail.

- **Best Practices** – things like the security of the website, defined image aspect ratios, working form fields, etc.

- **SEO** – whether your site follows basic search engine optimization advice, which improves its usability.

You want to have as high a score as possible in all four of the categories. Performance is the toughest one, and the one that is most affected by the Core Web Vitals. Accessibility, Best Practices and SEO can all be handled through the use of your Content Management System. Performance is more tricky because it could involve tuning some things on the server, the use of Content Distribution Networks, and other technical items that you may not be comfortable doing.

One thing you can do that will make the process of improving your performance score easier is to make sure you have high quality hosting. If you run your website on WordPress, like I recommend, use a hosting company that specializes in WordPress. Don't skimp on your hosting.

Google provides all this information separately for desktop and mobile. It is important to rank well in both areas, but if one is more important than the other, it's mobile. Optimize for mobile first. Google will test your site as if it is being viewed on a 3G network. This means it will be much slower than what most of your users will actually experience in real life. It's all about making your site as easy to use as possible for as many visitors as possible, regardless of what kind of device or Internet connection they have.

For each of the items discussed above, Google will provide a list of diagnostics that tell you what the problems are. It's fairly technical stuff, so this may be an area where you will want to enlist the help of someone experienced in dealing with these matters.

You should test your site regularly to make sure your scores are good, and make adjustments as necessary to raise your scores.

Links

Link building is the process of acquiring backlinks from other websites to your website. Content is number one, but backlinks are also important for improving the visibility and ranking of your website in search engines. Here are some strategies for building backlinks for your website:

- **Content Creation.** This is always where you should start. Create high-quality, relevant content that other websites would be interested in linking to, and that people would be interested in sharing. Examples of such content could include informative blog posts about your town, your business, your employees, other businesses around town, etc.; infographics; videos; and interactive tools related to travel and hospitality. You will create much of this content during the "marketing by walking around" process.

- **Guest Posting.** You should post original content on your own website, but it can be a great idea to try and get content on other sites as well. Reach out to other websites that are a good fit and offer to write a guest post for their website. In exchange, include a link back to your website in the author bio or within the content. Are there restaurants in your town that have website blogs? That is a natural fit for a hotel, and vice versa. People who stay in hotels will be looking for places to eat.

- **Directory Listings.** List your website on relevant directories and travel websites. If you are a hotel, you're probably already listed on sites like TripAdvisor, Booking.com, or Hotels.com. These sites often provide backlinks to your website, which can help improve your visibility and search engine ranking. Look for other less obvious places for links as well.

- **Social Media Marketing.** Promote your website on social media platforms and encourage your followers to share your content. I put my clients' URLs on almost every social media post I do. When other users share your content, it can help spread the word about your business and create backlinks to your website. We talk a lot more about this below.

- **Local Citations.** List your business information, such as the name, address, and phone number, on local business directories and maps. Yelp is an obvious example. This can help improve your visibility in local search results. We go into more detail about local SEO later.

- **Partnership and Collaboration.** Partner with other hotels, travel agencies, restaurants or other websites in your industry to promote each other's services. This can lead to backlinks from these websites to your hotel's website.

Link building is a grind. It is a long-term strategy that requires patience and persistence. It is generally best to avoid strategies like direct one-to-one link swaps or purchasing links. If you do decide to buy links, they should be very high quality and from quality, relevant websites – which means they won't be cheap!

Guest Posting

Guest posting is writing an article for another website (not your own) in order to get a link back to your site and a little blurb about your business. Full disclosure: I don't do a lot of this. I concentrate my efforts mostly on content for MY clients' sites. That's where I want my best content to reside. However, guest posting can be an effective way to generate links, so it might be something you want to try. To find websites to do a guest post, you can follow these steps:

- **Know Your Audience.** Determine who your target audience is and what type of websites they frequent. This can include travel blogs, local news websites, or industry-specific websites.

- **Do Your Research.** Use Google search or third-party research tools to find websites that rank for keywords related to your business and target audience. This can help you identify websites that would be interested in your content and open to publishing a guest post. You likely already know some local websites that would be good candidates.

- **Look for High DA Sites.** As much as possible, look for websites with high Domain Authority (DA). DA is a metric that measures the quality and credibility of a website. Websites with a high DA score provide more value to your website. However, when doing posts for local websites, you may not find a whole lot that have high DA scores. That is alright.

- **Check Guest Post Guidelines.** Once you have identified a few potential websites, check if they accept guest posts and if they have guidelines for guest posting. Some websites may have specific requirements for content length, format, or subject matter.

- **Reach Out to Website Owners.** Reach out to the owners of the websites you are interested in and introduce yourself and your business. Explain why you would like to guest post on their website and what you can offer their audience. Offer to write a high-quality article that provides value to their audience and includes a link back to your website.

Another option rather than requesting a guest post is to just go ahead and post something about the other business, such as a review. I do this often. Let's say you manage a hotel, and you write a review of a local restaurant. Include a link to the restaurant in the article, then contact that restaurant and let them know about the review, and that they might want to post something about it. Even if they just post a link to a social media profile, that is still one more link for you, and a little bit of social media visibility for your business. Every little bit helps!

By following these steps and consistently creating high-quality content, you can build relationships with other websites and businesses, and create valuable backlinks to your website.

Domain Authority

Domain Authority (DA), mentioned above, is a search engine ranking score, on a scale from 1 to 100, developed by a company called Moz. It is accepted as one of the best measures of how well a website would expect to rank in Google. As such, it is a good gage of websites from which to pursue a backlink.

Moz is a paid service, so if you want to see actual Domain Authority scores, you will have to sign up for an account at moz.com.

There are other services that also score websites in a very similar fashion, some of which are free. One to try is ahrefs.com/site-audit. Just type in the domain name and it will provide a score. Yet another option is Semrush, which offers a free trial.

Moz, ahrefs and Semrush are paid services if you want to use the tools they make available to improve your own site's authority rankings.

How to Increase Domain Authority

Domain Authority is calculated based on a variety of factors, including the number and quality of inbound links pointing to a website, the relevance of the content on the website, and the website's overall trustworthiness and authority in its industry.

Here are some strategies for improving your Domain Authority.

Build high-quality inbound links

One of the most important factors in determining Domain Authority is the quality and quantity of inbound links pointing to a website. In the hospitality industry, there are a number of ways to build these links. Being involved with other businesses and events in your town provide you an opportunity to create some very high-quality inbound links. Refer to the list above for some link-building strategies.

Not all links are created equal. Google's algorithm places greater weight on links from authoritative websites with relevant content. So it's important to focus on building high-quality links from trustworthy sources. Avoid low quality, junk links.

Create high-quality, relevant content

Another important factor in increasing Domain Authority is creating high-quality, relevant content on your website. This means producing blog posts, articles, and other content that is valuable to your target audience and reflects the expertise of your business.

For example, a hotel might create blog posts about local attractions, travel tips, or guest experiences. A restaurant might publish articles about local food trends or recipes inspired by their menu. By producing content that is relevant and valuable to your audience, you can attract inbound links and improve your website's overall authority. Plus, Google really likes seeing outbound links from your website to other sites. We will talk more about this below.

Improve website speed and user experience

Google's algorithm also takes into account website speed and user experience when determining search rankings. This means it's important to ensure that your website loads quickly and provides a positive user experience.

Some ways to improve website speed and user experience include optimizing images, using a content delivery network (CDN) to distribute content more quickly, and ensuring that your website is mobile-friendly and accessible to users with disabilities.

Refer back to the section on Google Core Web Vitals for more information.

Earn social media shares and engagement

Finally, social media can be a powerful tool for increasing Domain Authority. When your content is shared and engaged with on social media platforms, it can earn valuable links and signal to search engines that your website is authoritative and relevant.

To encourage social media shares and engagement, it's important to create and share high-quality, shareable content on your social media channels. This might include sharing blog posts, images, videos, or other content that showcases your business's unique offerings and expertise.

It's also important to engage with your social media followers and respond to their comments and questions in a timely and helpful manner. This can help build trust and loyalty among your audience and encourage them to share and engage with your content more frequently.

By focusing on building high-quality inbound links, creating relevant and valuable content, optimizing for local search, improving website speed and user experience, and earning social media shares and engagement, you can increase your Domain Authority and establish your business as a trusted and authoritative presence in your industry.

Google Search Console

You will want to create a Google Search Console (previously known as Google Webmaster Tools) account for your website. The Google Search Console is a free tool provided by Google that helps website owners monitor and maintain their website's presence in Google search results.

By setting up a Google Search Console account, you can make informed decisions to improve your website's visibility and ranking in Google search results.

Here are the steps to set up a Google Search Console account at the time of this writing:

- **Create a Google Account.** If you don't already have a Google account, you'll need to create one to use the Google Search Console. Go to google.com and click the Sign in button. On the next page, click Create account.

- **Visit the Google Search Console Website.** Go to **search.google.com/search-console** to access the Google Search Console.

- **Add Your Website.** Click on the "Start Now" button and enter the URL of your website.

- **Verify Ownership.** To verify that you are the owner of the website, you will need to add a verification code to your website or use Google's recommended method of verification. Whoever manages your website and hosting should be able to take care of it.

- **Submit Your Sitemap.** Once your website is verified, you can submit your sitemap to Google. A sitemap is a file in XML format that lists the pages on your website you want Google to crawl and helps Google navigate and understand the structure of your website. The sitemap will be a page on your website, so you will supply Google the URL to that page. Your website content management system (such as WordPress) should have a way to create your sitemap automatically.

Here is how to use Google Search Console to improve your search rankings:

- **Monitor Performance.** You can see how your website is performing in Google search results, including the number of clicks, impressions, and average position for each search query. To view this data, click the Performance button.

- **Identify Technical Issues.** Google Search Console can alert you to any technical issues with your website, such as crawl errors, security issues, and mobile compatibility issues. Click Core Web Vitals for issues that are affecting your rankings, as discussed above. Click Mobile Usability to learn if Google is having problems with the usability of your website on mobile devices, which can greatly affect your search visibility.

- **Improve Your Website's Visibility.** You can use the data from Google Search Console to make informed decisions about the content and structure of your website, including keyword optimization and internal linking strategies, to improve your website's visibility in Google search results.

For example, maybe you see that you are on page 3 for the search term "San Fransisco coffee donuts" and that you get some amount of traffic from it. Pushing that ranking up to page 2, and then page 1, would greatly increase that traffic. Therefore it would make sense to focus some SEO effort on that keyword.

Note: technically there aren't really numbered search pages any more. Google just displays more results as you scroll down the page. However you look at it, the higher up you are, the better.

- **Monitor Your Backlinks.** You can see a list of the websites linking to your website and monitor the quality of these links to ensure they are helping to boost your website's visibility in Google search results. Click the Links button on the main menu to view this information.

- **Check Indexing.** Learn if Google is having trouble indexing any of the pages on your website. If there are pages not being indexed (that should), you can identify them and figure out what the problem is. You want to make sure Google is able to index all pages that you want to be discovered in searches.

You really just need to create your account and get in there and click around. You will learn all kinds of things about your website performance. You can even win little awards as your search traffic reaches various milestones. Goofy but fun.

Google Search Console is an invaluable tool for improving your website's performance. It is very likely that your competitors are not taking advantage of this tool, so you should! In general, you should make use of everything Google makes available. It will provide the roadmap for success getting search traffic to your website.

Chapter 4: Social Media

We've been plowing through some technical details – stuff that honestly isn't all that much fun to deal with, but things that are essential for good search engine visibility. It's the infrastructure that has to be built for your marketing campaigns. But now let's talk about something more fun – getting social!

Social media platforms provide a large and engaged audience, allowing your business to reach and connect with potential customers, promote your brand, and increase awareness about your offerings. You can use platforms like Facebook, Instagram, X, and LinkedIn to share engaging content, run targeted advertisements, and interact with guests. Additionally, social media can also serve as a customer service channel, helping you to manage guest inquiries and feedback in real-time.

Once you've got all the infrastructure discussed earlier in place, it's time to get cranking on your social media.

Facebook

I highly recommend that Facebook become a staple of your social media campaign. It does not have the youngest audience, but it contains a very large percentage of the main market you want – people with money!

Here is a basic Facebook marketing plan:

- **Create a Facebook Business Page.** A hotel or restaurant should create a Facebook Business

Page that accurately represents its brand and provides useful information such as location, contact details, and services offered. To create a business Page, click the dots at the top of the main menu, then select Create / Page. Then fill out ALL the information Facebook asks for. If you have a well-fleshed-out Page, you are more likely to receive visibility in the Facebook network.

FYI, Facebook Pages do not have logins. When you create a Page, you become its administrator, but you can assign administrative power (as well as other levels of rights) to anyone you want.

- **Share Engaging Content on a Regular Basis.** Share visually appealing photos and videos of your business, its rooms and amenities (for hotels), items on your menu (for restaurants), and information about the surrounding area. Highlight special offers, events, and promotions to keep followers engaged and informed. We will discuss this more below.

- **Use Facebook Ads.** Facebook has excellent targeting capabilities. Utilize Facebook's targeting options to reach specific audiences, such as those interested in travel or those who have recently searched for hotels or restaurants in a particular location. You can boost content posts to your Page, or create standalone advertisements. It can be hard to get started building a following, so running ads is a way to kickstart the process.

- **Engage with Followers.** Respond to comments and messages from followers, and create conversations around topics relevant to your business, your location, or anything else that your audience will find interesting.

  A popular post may end up with MANY comments, and it can be difficult to stay on top of them all. That is another good reason to assign administrative privileges to someone who can be responsible for responding to them.

- **Monitor Analytics.** Regularly monitor the performance of your Facebook page using Facebook Insights to understand what is working and what can be improved.

That's it in a nutshell. It ain't rocket science – but it ain't easy! It requires persistence. It requires regularity. If you want to be successful with Facebook (or any of the social media platforms), then you need to post content almost every day.

Coming up with new content every day is hard. I suggest you mix it up. Here are some types of content that can be effective:

- **Visual Content.** High-quality photos and videos showcasing your business – for a hotel, it starts with rooms, amenities, and surrounding area; for a restaurant, the interior, food, customers, etc. But don't be shy to walk way outside your own borders, as we will discuss.

- **Behind-the-scenes Content.** Offer a behind-the-scenes look at what goes into running your business, such as staff training sessions, housekeeping procedures, or kitchen operations. You very likely have some real characters working for you. Let those personalities shine through! It's good marketing for customers to feel like they already know the people who work for you.

- **Customer Testimonials.** Share positive reviews, ratings, and comments from guests, to build trust and credibility with potential customers. One thing I like to do is combine a testimonial with a beautiful image of the business. It makes for great visual content.

- **Special Offers and Promotions.** Announce exclusive deals and promotions, such as seasonal packages, early bird discounts, or loyalty rewards.

- **Local Attractions and Events.** Highlight local attractions, events, and activities to provide value to guests and showcase your location. You want people coming into your town to take part in events so that they can also enjoy your business. Find out what bands are playing in town. What nightclubs are happening. Talk about any holiday-related events. Basically anything that is anything that a visitor to your town might want to do.

- **Reviews of Other Businesses.** I do this a lot. For example, for my hotel clients, I will post restaurant reviews. When you have done enough of those, you can then compile them into a local restaurant guide. Your website then becomes even more of a resource for visitors coming into town.

- **Industry News and Trends.** Share news and information relevant to your industry, such as travel tips, tourism statistics, or emerging technologies. Did you town just get voted one of the 10 best small towns in your state? Create a post about it! Find things to brag about.

- **Contests.** Facebook recently relaxed the rules about contests, so it is easier to do than it used to be. However, it is much easier to pull off an effective, professional-looking contest with a third part service. One I have used that I like is Gleam.io. Not a paid endorsement. There are lots of options. The benefit of a platform like Gleam is that it sets up the contest so that the entrants get more chances by performing certain tasks that help spread news of the contest. It has a viral effect. But however you do it, a contest is a great way to get a ton of free eyeballs.

By posting a mix of these types of content, you can keep your social media followers engaged and informed, and build a strong online presence. Once again, just to be clear – YOU MUST DO THIS STUFF ALMOST EVERY DAY.

Instagram

Instagram and Facebook are both social media platforms, but there are some key differences between the two:

- **Visual Focus.** Instagram is heavily focused on visual content, such as photos and videos, whereas Facebook is suited for a wider range of content types, including text, links, articles, and live videos.

- **Demographics.** Instagram has a younger demographic, with a higher concentration of users in the 18-29 age range, while Facebook has a wider age range and a more diverse user base.

- **Content and Engagement.** Instagram emphasizes aesthetics and creativity, and users tend to engage more with visually appealing content, while Facebook prioritizes connections with friends and family and allows for more in-depth engagement through features such as comments, groups, and events.

- **Advertisements.** Both platforms offer advertising opportunities, but the types of ads and targeting options can differ. Instagram has a more visual format and tends to be used for brand building and image-based promotions, while Facebook offers more advanced targeting options and is often used for direct response and conversion-focused campaigns.

You can use Instagram for marketing by following these steps:

- **Create a Strong Profile.** Establish a visually appealing and professional Instagram profile that accurately represents your business and its brand.

- **Share High-Quality Visual Content.** Share visually stunning photos and videos of your business and its operations, and surrounding area. Use hashtags to increase visibility and reach a wider audience.

- **Engage with Followers.** Respond to comments and messages from followers, and create conversations around topics relevant to the hospitality industry. Use Instagram's "Stories" and "IGTV" features to share behind-the-scenes content and offer a unique perspective.

- **Collaborate with Influencers and Partners.** Partner with local influencers, travel bloggers, and other relevant brands to reach a wider audience and increase brand awareness.

- **Use Instagram Ads.** Utilize Instagram's advertising platform to reach specific audiences and promote specific offers or packages. Instagram's visually-driven format makes it well-suited for image-based ads and promotions.

Any time you post a photo on your Facebook news stream, post it to Instagram as well. There are social media management tools that allow you to post to multiple sites at the same time, which is a good idea. We will list some of the more popular options later.

Pinterest

Pinterest can be a useful platform for hotel and restaurant marketing. Pinterest is a visual discovery and planning platform that allows users to save and organize ideas for their future plans, such as travel. Hotels can take advantage of this by creating boards that showcase their offerings, such as room types, amenities, and local attractions. You can share travel inspiration and tips related to your location, making it easier for users to discover and plan their next trip.

By creating engaging and informative content on Pinterest, you can reach potential guests who are actively planning and researching their travel plans.

Additionally, Pinterest's audience tends to have high purchasing power and be more engaged with brand content, making it an effective platform for hospitality marketing.

Here are some ways to use Pinterest for your marketing:

- **Create Visually Stunning Boards.** Create boards that showcase your offerings, such as rooms, amenities, menu items, local attractions, and other interesting local businesses. Use high-quality images and descriptive captions to highlight the unique aspects of your business and its location.

- **Share Travel Inspiration.** Share travel inspiration boards, highlighting the best things to do in the area, scenic destinations, and interesting activities. This can help potential guests discover you as well as helping them plan their trip.

- **Utilize Keywords and Hashtags.** Use keywords and hashtags in the captions and boards to increase the visibility of your content and make it easier for users to find.

- **Partner with Influencers.** Partner with travel influencers and bloggers to reach a wider audience and increase your exposure.

- **Promote Special Offers.** Share special offers and promotions on Pinterest, and consider running Pinterest Ads to reach specific audiences and drive bookings.

Every time you post a piece of content somewhere on the Internet, it is one more way for someone to stumble onto you. Facebook, Instagram and Pinterest are three distinct ways to pull users into your circle.

They're certainly not the only social media options. Currently I'm experimenting with TikTok. Would that be right for your business? It depends on who your market is. It has a very young audience. TikTok is quite different from the above options. I will be posting my thoughts about its effectiveness at workmedia.net, so feel free to check back over there to learn more.

It can be difficult to keep up with the various social media accounts with which you will need to work. There are a number of platforms in the market that make the process easier. Using one of these tools, you can upload your media once and upload it to multiple locations. Some of them also make it easier to stay on top of comments left on your posts. I list several of these in the resources section at the end of the book.

It bears repeating – you have to do this over and over again. Monday through Friday, and sometimes on the weekend too. And you can't repeat content, or at least not very often. That's boring. You can't be boring.

The result of all this is that you will have steady growth, and occasionally you will have a piece of content explode. When that happens, you need to take a close look at what happened. What was it about the piece that made it so popular? Is it something you can replicate? If you can identify what it was, then that becomes a template for use on future updates.

Unfortunately, very often the answer to what it made it so popular is "nothing." I have posted VERY similar content on different occasions, and one exploded while the other barely moved the needle. I often cannot identify what it is about the one that did so well. But that's why you have to just keep doing it constantly and consistently.

Personally, I think it's fun when combined with the secret sauce we discuss later.

Chapter 5: Paid Search

Paid search marketing involves placing ads on search engines such as Google, Bing, and Yahoo. These ads are triggered by specific keywords. They appear at the top of or around the organic results on a search results page, making them highly visible to users searching for related information.

By using paid search marketing, a hotel or restaurant can reach potential guests who are actively searching for information about food, lodging, travel, and related topics. You can target ads to specific keywords and locations, ensuring that you reach the most relevant audience.

Paid search marketing allows for real-time tracking and measurement, allowing you to adjust your campaigns and refine your targeting strategies to maximize results. That is a HUGE advantage over traditional marketing media. Once a print ad is published, it is published. It will always look the same to whoever looks at the ad. TV and radio ads are expensive to change. Paid search ads can be changed any time.

Overall, paid search marketing can be an effective tool to help you drive bookings and reach potential guests. However, it is important to have a well-planned and executed strategy to maximize results and achieve a positive return on investment.

The cost of paid search marketing can vary depending on several factors, such as:

- **Competition.** The cost of a given keyword or ad placement can be affected by the level of competition for that keyword. Keywords that are in high demand and have a lot of competition will generally be more expensive.

- **Budget.** The more you are willing to spend, the more visibility and reach you can achieve through paid search marketing. Budgets can be moved up and down instantly, giving you a ton of control over your spend.

- **Keyword Quality Score.** The Quality Score of a keyword is a rating of its relevance and quality, and it affects the cost of the keyword. Keywords with a higher Quality Score generally cost less to advertise.

- **Location.** The location of your business and your target audience can also impact the cost of paid search marketing. For example, advertising in a densely populated city may be more expensive than in a rural area.

Your clicks may cost a few cents, or they could cost several dollars per click, depending on the factors mentioned above.

Word of caution: Google knows how to make that money. It didn't become the monster it is today by being shy about taking money. So make sure you analyze your results as you go so you spend money on the things that are working. Also, you may receive calls from Google representatives offering to help you with your account. It is fine to have the call and listen to their advice, but be careful what you do. There have been times when my paid search results have DECLINED as a result of implementing their advice. And again, be careful about your spend, at least at first.

Done correctly, a well-executed and optimized paid search campaign can result in a high return on investment for the hotel or restaurant, making it a cost-effective way to reach potential guests and drive bookings.

Advertising Platforms

If you can only use one paid search platform, it is recommended to use Google Ads, as it is the largest and most widely used search engine in the world. Google Ads provides a broad range of targeting options, allowing you to reach potential guests who are actively searching for information related to travel, lodging or dining. Additionally, Google Ads has a large network of partner sites, which increases the visibility and reach of your ads.

By using Google Ads, you can reach a large and diverse audience and drive bookings through your website. Additionally, Google Ads provides robust tracking and measurement tools, allowing you to monitor the performance of your campaigns and make data-driven decisions to optimize your results.

You can sign up for Google Ads at **ads.google.com**.

Google Ads is a versatile and effective platform for hospitality businesses, and can provide a strong return on investment when done well. It also has about 90% of all search traffic. However, there are other options. The number one alternative in the search engine world is Bing.

Bing is the search engine owned by Microsoft. Obviously, if Google gets 90% of all search traffic, then Bing has much less. However, it has one big advantage, which is that you will likely pay less per click. It will be just as targeted and cost less. It could even be more targeted than Google if, for example, you cater to an older demographic. Bing reaches a somewhat older market, as well as a higher income market.

Ads on Bing are called Microsoft Ads. To sign up to give it a try, visit **ads.microsoft.com**.

Yet another paid search option is Yahoo!. Yahoo! receives slightly less traffic than Bing but is certainly worth a try as well. Feel free to experiment with different paid search options until you find what provides the best return on investment. Maybe it's Google, maybe not.

Paid Search Marketing Plan

We're not going to go into great detail about setting up a paid search campaign. We could easily fill this book with just that information. But here is a sample plan demonstrating how a hotel in a tourist location could use Google Ads to drive traffic to its website and book reservations:

- **Set Up Your Account**. Visit **ads.google.com** to set up your Google Ads account. You will need a credit card for payment (you will only be charged once some click costs have accrued).

- **Define the Target Audience.** Determine who the hotel's ideal guests are based on demographics, interests, and behaviors. For example, the hotel may want to target couples in their 30s who enjoy outdoor activities and have a higher income. Or maybe it caters mostly to business travelers. As much as possible, try to define who your most profitable target market is.

- **Identify Relevant Keywords.** Research and identify the most relevant and high-traffic keywords that people are searching for when looking for a hotel in the tourist town. Examples could include "romantic hotel in [town name]," "hotel near [tourist attraction]," or "luxury hotel in [town name]." Use Google's Keyword Planner tool to do this research.

- **Develop Ad Copy.** Create compelling ad copy that highlights the hotel's unique features and benefits, such as its location, amenities, and customer service. Use the identified keywords in the ad copy and make sure it aligns with the target audience's interests. It is also perfectly acceptable to review ads from competing properties and borrow ideas from that. If you want to take that a step further, you can use a service like **SpyFu.com** to analyze the most successful ads in your category.

- **Set Up Landing Pages.** Create specific landing pages on the hotel's website that align with the ads and offer a clear call-to-action, such as "book now" or "learn more." These landing pages should be optimized for conversions and provide a seamless user experience. For example, if you have a Valentine's Day special that you are promoting via paid ads, you should link those ads to a page that talks specifically about that promotion.

- **Set Up Conversion Tracking.** This can be a little complicated depending on how your website works. The idea is that when someone books a room, you want to report that information to Google Ads (as well as Google Analytics or whatever analytics platform you use).

- **Set Up Google Ads Campaigns.** Set up campaigns based on the identified keywords and target audience. Use relevant targeting options, such as location, interests, and behaviors.

- **Optimize Ad Campaigns.** Regularly review and optimize the ad campaigns to ensure maximum effectiveness. This includes adjusting ad copy, keywords, and bidding strategies based on performance metrics, such as click-through rate, conversion rate, and cost per acquisition. This is where having conversion tracking set up REALLY helps you better manage your account, because you will actually know what is working in dollar terms.

- **Retarget Website Visitors.** Set up retargeting campaigns to reach people who have previously visited the hotel's website but did not book a reservation. Use personalized ad copy and offers to entice them to return and complete a reservation.

- **Monitor and Analyze Performance.** Continuously monitor and analyze the performance of the ad campaigns to identify opportunities for improvement and optimization. Use data to inform future campaigns and strategies.

By following these steps, a hotel in a tourist town can use Google Ads to drive targeted traffic to its website and increase reservations. It's important to keep in mind that this is an ongoing process that requires regular monitoring and optimization to ensure maximum effectiveness.

For a restaurant, the process is basically the same. One difference is that you may not be actually selling anything on your website. In this case, you may still want to create some kind of offer that will allow you to track performance.

For example, you could run ads that mention a coupon code that can be used to save 20% on your meal. You will know from the number of people who use that coupon whether or not your ad is being effective.

You can also just run ads without regard for any kind of conversion tracking, focusing more on traffic. Driving targeted traffic to your website will always improve your visibility and improve your chance of picking up new business.

This was an abbreviated overview of paid search. The subject can get quite complicated, so you will want to either:

1. Hire a professional to manage your campaigns; or
2. Put some real time into learning what you are doing.

Don't just throw up some ads and hope for the best. Make sure you have everything set up properly. I highly advise you have conversion tracking in place. Start with a small budget and grow the campaign as you generate data and learn what works.

Paid search is not necessary to engage in marketing by walking around. If you are starting from scratch and have no traffic and no following, it is a great way to start driving traffic. But the marketing by walking around approach is much more about spending sweat equity than it is spending money.

Chapter 6: Email

Email marketing is a powerful tool for hospitality businesses to reach and engage with their target audience and drive bookings. Here are some ways hotels can effectively use email marketing:

- **Build an Email List.** Start by building a list of subscribers who have expressed an interest in your business and its offerings. This can be done through sign-ups on your website, at check-in, on your Facebook Page, or through other promotions and events. You are also allowed to add your customers to your list. If someone has done business with you, they get on the list.

- **Personalize Communications.** As much as possible, personalize communications to each subscriber, using his or her name, location, and other relevant information. This will make the email feel more relevant and targeted, increasing the chances of engagement.

- **Share Valuable Content.** Share valuable content with subscribers, such as promotions, special offers, travel tips, and news about your business and its location. This keeps you front-of-mind with your subscribers. When they are looking for a place to stay or eat, you will be on their minds.

- **Segment the List.** If possible, segment the email list based on subscriber preferences, past history with your business, and other relevant factors. This will allow you to send targeted and relevant communications to each subscriber, increasing the chances of engagement and conversion.

- **Measure and Optimize.** Use analytics and tracking tools to monitor the performance of the email campaigns and optimize them over time. For example, there could be a certain time of day that results in more opens. This will help you continually improve your email marketing results and drive more bookings.

- **Try to Have a Theme.** Holidays are obvious examples. I will do a Christmas or Winter issue that talks about upcoming events – parades, Santa Claus events, etc. It can be difficult to create a newsletter, so having a theme can give you direction and help you flesh out the content.

The frequency of email communications will depend on various factors, including the subscribers' preferences and your goals. However, here are some general guidelines:

- **Monthly Newsletters.** A monthly newsletter is a great way to keep subscribers informed and engaged with your business and its offerings. This type of email can include promotions, special offers, travel tips, and other relevant content.

- **Promotional Emails.** Promotional emails, such as special offers and discounts, can be sent out more frequently, such as every 2-4 weeks. However, it's important to strike a balance between keeping subscribers engaged and avoiding over-communication.

- **Transactional Emails.** Transactional emails, such as confirmation emails and post-stay follow-ups, should be sent out as needed, and can be customized for each individual subscriber based on their preferences and booking history.

It's important to remember that the frequency of email communications can vary depending on the target audience and their preferences. The key is to find a frequency that works best for your specific audience and goals, and to regularly review and adjust the frequency based on the performance of the campaigns.

Here are some examples of effective content for an email newsletter:

- **Photos.** As will be discussed shortly, you are going to be taking a TON of photos. Use some of your best photos in your newsletter. Mixing nice looking photos into the text content breaks it up and makes it more visually interesting. However, keep in mind that you don't want to send an email that is extremely large in file size, so make sure to resize your photos to a size appropriate for email.

- **Promotions and Special Offers.** Share exclusive promotions and special offers with subscribers, such as discounts on room rates, meal specials, packages, spa services, etc.

- **Travel Tips and Inspiration.** Provide travel tips and inspiration to subscribers, such as recommendations for local attractions and activities, dining options, and more.

- **News and Updates.** Share news and updates about your business, such as new amenities and services, events and promotions, and renovations or expansions.

- **Behind-the-Scenes.** Give subscribers a behind-the-scenes look at your business, such as photos and stories from the staff, guests, and local community.

- **User-Generated Content.** Share user-generated content, such as photos and testimonials from previous customers, to showcase your offerings and highlight the positive experiences of others.

- **Seasonal Content.** Provide seasonal content, such as holiday greetings, summer travel tips, and winter getaway ideas, to keep subscribers engaged and informed throughout the year.

- **Article content from your website.** I do this often. It just makes sense to use your content as many ways as you can. I usually only post a couple of paragraphs of the article and then link to the article page on my client's website.

Incorporating a mix of these types of content will keep your newsletter interesting.

Here's an example of a template for a hospitality email newsletter that can be used to promote your business and keep your guests engaged:

[Header Image: Use an eye-catching image of your business or a local attraction to grab the reader's attention]

[Opening Greeting: Start your email with a friendly greeting to your guests, such as "Hello from [Business Name]"]

[Opening Paragraph: Use the opening paragraph to provide an update or announcement about your business, such as a new amenity, service, menu item or event. Be sure to highlight the value of the update and how it benefits your guests.]

[Photo]

[Body Section 1: Use this section to highlight a local attraction or event that may be of interest to your guests. Include details about the attraction, including its

location, hours, and any special offers or discounts available to your hotel guests.]

[Photo]

[Body Section 2: Some kind of less promotional content. It could be an article from your website, or a snippet of the article with a link to your website. It can be anything that your subscribers might find interesting.]

[Photo]

[Body Section 3: A different type of content. You could place an image that links to a video on your YouTube channel. Or it could be a contest announcement. Anything fun and interesting.]

[Call-to-Action: Use a clear call-to-action to encourage your guests to take action, such as "Book Now," "Learn More," or "Visit Our Website." Include a hyperlink to your website or booking page to make it easy for guests to take action.]

[Closing Greeting: End your email with a friendly closing greeting, such as "Thanks for reading our newsletter! We will see you soon!"]

[Footer: Include a footer that includes your hotel's contact information, social media links, and an option for guests to unsubscribe from your email list.]

In general, you want to keep your email newsletter concise, focused, and easy to read. Use attention-grabbing images, clear calls-to-action, and targeted content to engage your subscribers and encourage them to take action. Don't be overly promotional. By providing real value and entertainment, you can build a loyal following who will look forward to your emails. Using a legitimate email delivery service will help take care of details like unsubscribe links.

Chapter 7: Local SEO

Local SEO is a type of search engine optimization that focuses on optimizing a business's online presence for a specific geographic location. For hospitality businesses, this is extremely important! People are going to be coming into your town and looking for places to stay and places to eat. When those people search on their phone or computer for such places, you want to be found. This means ensuring that your website is optimized for search queries related to your location and the services you offer.

One way to do this is by optimizing your Google Business profile, which can help your business appear in local search results and on Google Maps. Make sure your profile is complete, accurate, and includes photos and reviews from satisfied customers. We go into more detail about this below.

You can also optimize your website's content and meta tags for local search queries. This might include including your location in your page titles, meta descriptions, and content, as well as using structured data markup to provide additional information about your business to search engines. Read more about structured data markup below.

Local SEO involves optimizing your website, online directories, and other digital assets to rank well in local search engine results pages (SERPs) for keywords related to your business and location.

Local SEO helps hotels reach potential customers who are searching for accommodations in the area where the hotel is located. For restaurants, it helps them attract hungry customers. By optimizing your website and other online assets for local search, you can improve your visibility and drive more relevant, local traffic to your website.

Now let's look at the local SEO process in more detail.

Local Optimization

Here are some steps to optimize your hotel website for local SEO:

- **Claim and Optimize your Google Business Profile.** Google Business Profile Manager is a free tool that allows businesses to manage their online presence across Google, including search and maps. Optimizing your Google Business Profile can help your business show up in relevant local search results and get discovered by nearby customers. It is a critical component of local SEO. Make sure to claim your profile and provide accurate, up-to-date information about your business, including its name, address, phone number, hours of operation, and photos.

- **Use Local Keywords.** Use keywords in your website's content and meta tags that reflect your hotel or restaurant's location and the services it offers. This will help search engines understand the context of your website and help it rank well in local search results.

- **Get Listed in Local Directories.** Get your hotel listed in local directories and online travel websites to help it reach potential customers in the area and help improve your Google local results positioning.

- **Encourage Customer Reviews.** Online reviews are a powerful factor in local search ranking, so encourage your customers to leave reviews on popular websites like TripAdvisor, Google Business, and Yelp.

- **Include Location Information on Your Website.** Make sure your website includes your hotel's complete address and contact information, as well as information about the local area, including popular attractions and landmarks. I recommend placing it in the footer so that it is on every page of your site.

- **Build Local Backlinks.** Build links from other local websites to your hotel website. These links can help search engines understand the relevance of your website for local search queries.

- **Use Schema Markup.** Use schema markup to help search engines understand the context of your website and to provide additional information about your hotel, such as its address and contact information.

Here is an example of schema markup for a hotel:

```
<script type="application/ld+json">
{
  "@context": "https://schema.org",
  "@type": "LodgingBusiness",
  "name": "The Grand Hotel",
  "address": {
    "@type": "PostalAddress",
    "streetAddress": "123 Main Street",
    "addressLocality": "Anytown",
    "addressRegion": "State",
    "postalCode": "Zip Code",
    "addressCountry": "Country"
  },
  "telephone": "+1-555-555-1212",
  "priceRange": "$$$",
  "image": "https://www.example.com/images/thegrandhotel.jpg",
```

```
  "amenities": [
    "Free Wi-Fi",
    "On-site Restaurant",
    "Fitness Center",
    "Spa and Wellness Center",
    "Room Service"
  ],
  "geo": {
    "@type": "GeoCoordinates",
    "latitude": "37.7749",
    "longitude": "-122.4194"
  }
}
</script>
```

This schema markup provides information about the Grand Hotel, including its name, address, telephone number, price range, amenities, and location. Schema markup helps search engines understand the context of your website and can improve its visibility in search results. The script would be placed in the head of your website.

By implementing these strategies, hotels can improve their visibility in local search results and reach more potential customers in their area.

Google Business Profile Manager

Google Business Profile Manager is a tool provided by Google that allows business owners to manage their business information that appears on Google search, including the Google Maps section. With Google Business Profile Manager, you can create a business profile that includes important details about your business, such as your business name, address, phone number, hours of operation, website, photos, and more.

To get up a Google Business Profile, visit **business.google.com**. Click the Add business button and follow the instructions. Remember that whatever information you set up here is exactly what people will see when they find you in Google local business results. So use this as another opportunity to showcase the best qualities of your business – how nice your rooms look, your location, items on your menu, etc.

Another interesting feature of Google Business Profile Manager is that it has a mini-blogging type of feature where you can add updates that also appear along with your business information. This is an opportunity most businesses miss. Use this feature. When you are doing your daily social media updates, include Google Business Profile. You can add a button to your posts that dials your phone when someone clicks on it, which you should do.

Google Business Profile Manager is where you can check and respond to reviews that people leave for your business in Google. You must respond to reviews – even the bad ones! In fact, it's more important to respond to any negative feedback. When you do that, avoid being defensive. Explain your side, apologize (if an apology is warranted) and be very polite.

Google Business Profile Manager also provides insights and analytics to help you understand how people are interacting with your business online. It will tell you things like how many people clicked on your business listing in Google and what search queries generated the most clicks.

Google Business Profile has a verification process. Google wants to make sure that you are an actual brick-and-mortar business conducting business at the address you specify. Just follow the directions for verification and you will be good to go.

By creating a Google Business Profile, you can ensure that your business information is accurate and up-to-date, and that it reaches a large audience of potential customers. Having a Google Business Profile can also improve your visibility in local search results, making it easier for potential customers to find you when searching for your type of business in your area.

Citations

Citations are references to your business's name, address, and phone number (NAP) on other websites, including directories, review sites, and social media platforms. These references can include links to your website but don't necessarily have to.

Citations help search engines like Google verify the accuracy of your NAP information. They also increase your visibility online and can drive more traffic to your website. The more high-quality citations your website has, the higher it is likely to appear in search engine results pages (SERPs) for relevant queries.

Why Are Citations Important?

Citations are a vital factor in local search engine optimization. As discussed above, local SEO is the practice of optimizing your online presence to attract customers from your local area, or who are visiting your local area. When people search for your type of business in your city or neighborhood, Google uses citations to determine the relevance and popularity of your site.

The quality and quantity of your citations impact your local search ranking. The more citations you have on relevant, authoritative websites, the more likely you are to rank higher in local search results. Citations also help establish you as a reputable and trustworthy business.

How Should You Use Citations?

To make the most of citations, you should focus on the following strategies:

- **Build High-Quality Citations.** Your hotel or restaurant should aim to build citations on authoritative, high-quality websites that are relevant to your business. These can include local directories, travel and tourism websites, and review sites like TripAdvisor or Yelp. The more relevant and authoritative the website, the more valuable the citation.

- **Consistency is Key.** Your hotel's NAP information should be consistent across all citations. This means that your hotel or restaurant's name, address, and phone number should be the same everywhere it is listed online. Inconsistencies can hurt your local search ranking and confuse customers looking for your hotel.

- **Monitor and Update Citations.** Regularly monitor your hotel's citations to ensure they are accurate and up-to-date. If you move to a new location or change your phone number, update your citations as soon as possible to avoid any confusion or negative impact on your local search ranking.

- **Use Local Keywords.** Include local keywords in your citations to help search engines understand your business's relevance to your local area. These keywords could include the name of your city or neighborhood, popular landmarks or attractions nearby, or local events.

- **Encourage Customer Reviews.** Encourage customers to leave reviews of your hotel or restaurant on review sites like TripAdvisor or Yelp. Positive reviews can help improve your hotel's online reputation and attract more customers. Make sure to respond to all reviews, both positive and negative, to show customers that you value their feedback.

Citations are an essential element of local SEO that can help improve your visibility and reputation online. By building high-quality citations, ensuring consistency, monitoring and updating your citations, using local keywords, and encouraging customer reviews, you can maximize the benefits of citations and outrank your competitors in search engine results pages.

Reviews

Citations and reviews are two distinct elements that play different roles in your online presence.

As discussed above, the primary purpose of citations is to provide search engines with consistent and accurate information about your NAP, which helps them verify your business's legitimacy and authority. Reviews, on the other hand, are customer feedback on websites like TripAdvisor, Yelp, and Google My Business. They typically include a star rating, written comments, and sometimes photos or videos.

The purpose of reviews is to provide potential customers with insights into the quality of your products or services. Positive reviews can help attract more customers, while negative reviews can hurt your business's reputation. You want to do everything you can to nurture positive reviews.

While citations and reviews serve different purposes, they are both critical elements of your online presence. Citations are important for local SEO and can help your business appear higher in search engine results pages for relevant queries. Plus, if there is somewhere where your competitors are listed, you want to be there too (or better yet, be there if they're not). Reviews are essential for your business's online reputation and can influence customers' decision-making processes.

It's important to note that search engines consider both citations and reviews when evaluating your online presence, and having a strong presence in both can help improve your visibility and attract more customers.

Popular Review Sites

You should aim to get reviews on platforms that are relevant to your business and popular among your target audience. Here are some platforms where you should try to get reviews:

- **Google Business Profile.** Google Business Profile Manager allows you to collect and respond to customer reviews, which can help improve your visibility and reputation. Refer to the section above for more specific information.

- **Yelp.** Yelp is a popular review site that allows users to search for businesses and read reviews from other travelers. Yelp also allows you to manage your listings, respond to reviews, and promote your business. You may already be listed in Yelp, in which case you will need to "claim" your business. If your business does not appear on Yelp, you can also add your business from scratch. To get started, visit yelp.com.

- **Facebook.** Facebook allows you to create a business Page where you can showcase your services, post updates, and interact with customers. Customers can also leave reviews on your Page, which can help improve your online reputation.

- **TripAdvisor.** TripAdvisor is one of the most popular review sites for hotels and restaurants and is known for its extensive database of user-generated reviews. TripAdvisor also allows you to manage your listings, respond to reviews, and promote your business. You will have to claim your listing or request a listing if you are not already there.

For hotels, there are a few directories that are specific to your industry:

- **Booking.com.** Booking.com is a popular booking site for hotels and also allows customers to leave reviews of their stay. Positive reviews on Booking.com can help attract more customers and improve your ranking on the platform.

- **Expedia.** Expedia is another popular booking site that allows customers to leave reviews of their stay. A hotel with positive reviews on Expedia can attract more customers and improve its online reputation.

How to Generate More Reviews

Here are some tactics you can use to encourage customers to leave more reviews:

- **Ask for Reviews.** This is a no-brainer. Encourage guests to leave a review of their experience by asking them in person, on their receipt, or in a follow-up email. Be sure to include links to relevant review sites to make it easy for guests to leave a review. It would even be a good idea to create some kind of card to leave with your customers politely requesting a review and providing basic instruction on how to do so.

- **Offer Incentives.** Consider offering a small incentive, such as a discount on their next stay (for hotels), or a free appetizer or drink at the bar (for restaurants), to guests who leave a review. Be sure to comply with relevant laws and regulations when offering incentives.

- **Provide Excellent Service.** Providing excellent service can go a long way in encouraging guests to leave positive reviews. Make sure your staff is friendly, knowledgeable, and helpful, and that your facilities are clean, comfortable, and well-maintained. It goes without saying, but people like to do business with other nice people. It's good business!

- **Display Review Sites.** Display logos or links to relevant review sites in your hotel lobby, on your website, or in your marketing materials. This will remind guests to leave a review and make it easy for them to do so.

- **Respond to Reviews.** Responding to reviews, both positive and negative, shows that you value your guests' feedback and are committed to providing excellent service. Responding to reviews can also encourage more guests to leave a review.

- **Use a Review Management Tool.** Consider using a review management tool like ReviewPro or Revinate to monitor your online reputation and manage your reviews more effectively. These tools can help you identify areas for improvement, respond to reviews more efficiently, and track your progress over time.

By using these tactics, you can encourage more guests to leave reviews and build a strong online reputation for your business. Remember to always comply with relevant laws and regulations and focus on providing excellent service to your guests.

Chapter 8: YouTube

YouTube is huge. You know that it is the world's largest video streaming platform. But you may not be aware that it is actually the second largest search engine after Google, which happens to own YouTube. YouTube gets about a billion views every day, and it is an excellent marketing platform for your business. By creating and sharing videos on YouTube, you can reach a wide audience and showcase your property, amenities, services, menu and your people. You can also showcase events happening around town and things outside the walls of your business.

Here are some benefits of using YouTube as a marketing platform for business:

- **Video Content is Engaging.** Video content can be more engaging and memorable than text or images alone. By creating high-quality videos that showcase your business, you can capture the attention of potential customers and increase their interest in your business.

- **Video Content is Shareable.** YouTube videos can be easily shared on social media, email, and other digital channels. By creating shareable videos that highlight the unique features of your hotel or restaurant, you can increase your reach and attract more customers.

- **YouTube is a Search Engine.** As mentioned above, YouTube is the second-largest search engine after Google, and many users use it to search for information about travel destinations, hotels, restaurants and attractions. By creating videos with relevant keywords and tags, you can improve your visibility and attract more customers. On top of videos appearing in YouTube search, they also appear in Web search results, so be strategic in your use of keywords in titles and descriptions.

- **YouTube is Cost-effective.** Creating and sharing videos on YouTube can be a cost-effective marketing strategy compared to other forms of digital marketing. With a smartphone or a basic camera and some editing software, you can create professional-looking videos without breaking the bank. Or you can take it up a notch and use something like I have, a Canon EOS R with an attached Shure condenser microphone.

To get started with YouTube, you need to create a channel. And "channel" is literally what it sounds like — it's your own TV channel where you create all the shows. Go to youtube.com, log in with your Google account, click on your logo in the upper right-hand corner, and then select the option to create a channel.

You should customize your channel by adding a picture (your logo, basically), a banner image that will show up on your channel, a description, handle, keywords, etc., all of which will help people find you on YouTube.

When you are ready to upload your first video, click the video upload button in the upper right-hand corner.

Video Content Ideas

Here are some ideas for the type of videos that you can create and share on YouTube:

- **Property Tour.** Showcase your hotel's property and amenities, including guest rooms, pool, spa, fitness center, and restaurant. If you are a restaurant, you might not have quite as much to tour, so just be creative.

- **Local Attractions.** Highlight nearby attractions, including popular landmarks, museums, restaurants, and nightlife. If there are mountains, go into the mountains. If there is a lake, go to the lake. If there is a famous landmark of any kind, go to it and take video and photos.

- **Guest Testimonials.** Feature guest testimonials to showcase the guest experience and promote your business.

- **Events.** Share videos of events held at your business, such as weddings, conferences, meetings and concerts.

- **Behind the Scenes.** Share behind-the-scenes videos that show the daily operations of your hotel, including housekeeping, kitchen, and front desk. Or have your chef talk about some of his favorite recipes.

Video Posting Guidelines

Here are some general guidelines to consider when planning your YouTube video strategy:

- **Quality Over Quantity.** In general, for videos that represent your business, it is more important to create high-quality content than to post videos frequently. Your videos should be well-produced, informative, and engaging, and should align with your brand and marketing goals.

  Having said that, there is also a place for quickly made, informal videos. Especially for the purpose of video shorts, it is very acceptable to casual in your approach. It really depends on who your audience is. If you do shorts, I recommend you also mix in some longer format videos as well.

- **Consistency is Key.** Consistency is important when it comes to building a following on YouTube. You should aim to post videos on a regular schedule, whether that's once a week, twice a month, or once per month. People who do YouTube professional post every day, and often multiple times per day. Unless you are willing to devote very significant time to YouTube, that is not reasonable for most of us. One high quality video per week is a good and reasonable goal.

- **Consider Your Audience.** Consider your target audience when planning your YouTube video strategy. Some audiences may prefer shorter, more frequent videos, while others may prefer longer, more in-depth videos. I recommend a mix of types of content – some longer format, higher quality; and some shorter, less formal quality.

- **Be Strategic.** Plan your YouTube video strategy around important events, seasons, and promotions. For example, you might create videos around holiday events or to promote seasonal packages.

- **Analyze Your Results.** Regularly review your YouTube analytics to determine what is working and what is not. This can help you adjust your strategy and create content that resonates with your target audience.

- **Monitor Comments.** You should also monitor your submissions for comments. YouTube has social media elements, such as the ability to have a conversation centered around a video's content. When people leave a comment, respond back as quickly as possible.

By being consistent, strategic, and analytical, you can create a successful YouTube video strategy that promotes your business and attracts more customers.

YouTube Analytics

YouTube Analytics provides data and insights into how your videos are performing, including information on views, engagement, and audience demographics.

To access YouTube Analytics, follow these steps:

- Log in to your YouTube account. Click your logo in the right-hand corner and select Creator Studio from the drop-down menu.

- Click on Analytics in the left-hand menu.

- You will see an overview of your channel's performance, including data on views, watch time, and subscribers.

- Click on any of the videos to view data about that specific video.

- Click on Comments to view comments, and promptly respond to anything legitimate.

Here are some of the key metrics you should look for in YouTube Analytics:

- **Views.** This metric shows the number of times your videos have been viewed.

- **Watch Time.** This metric shows the total amount of time viewers have spent watching your videos.

- **Subscribers.** This metric shows your subscriber count, and how your subscribers have grown over time.

- **Audience.** Information related to the age, gender, and location of your audience.

- **Research.** This page in your channel analytics lets you perform research to uncover the top searches for which you should be creating content.

By analyzing this data, you can determine which videos are performing well and which are not and adjust your strategy accordingly. For example, if you notice that a certain type of video is getting more views and engagement than others, you may want to create more videos of that type.

Similarly, if you notice that your audience is primarily located in a specific location, you may want to create content that appeals to that area.

It is also a great idea to research popular videos in your category and see if there are any ideas you could borrow. Don't COPY them, but there is nothing wrong with creating videos on similar subjects.

You can create much of your YouTube video material in the course of "marketing by walking around"...which we will discuss shortly.

That video material can also be recycled in a number of ways. For instance, you could cut out a smaller portion of the video to upload as a short on YouTube, Facebook and other platforms. TikTok is another option. Use your material in as many different ways as possible.

Chapter 9: Analytics

If you're gonna do all this work, then you might as well make sure you have an idea of how you're doing. Implementing Google Analytics (GA4) on your website can provide valuable insights into your website's performance, user behavior, and traffic sources. Here's a high-level explanation of how to implement GA4 on your website:

- **Set Up a Google Analytics Account.** To get started, you will need to set up a Google Analytics account by visiting **google.com/analytics**. This will require creating a Google account and linking it to your website.

- **Create a GA4 Property.** Once you have set up your Google Analytics account, you will need to create a GA4 property for your hotel website. You can have multiple GA4 properties in the same account. If you only have one business, then you will likely only need one GA4 property. If you have multiple locations with their own websites, you will want to set up a property for each one. This will require adding a new property in your Google Analytics account and selecting the GA4 option. GA4 is being phased out, so by the time you read this it will likely be the only option.

- **Add the GA4 Tracking Code.** To begin collecting data, you will need to add the GA4 tracking code to every page on your website that you want to track. One way to do this is by copying and pasting a code snippet provided by Google Analytics into the header of your website.

- **Set Up Conversion Tracking.** To track conversions, such as bookings or form submissions, you will need to set up conversion tracking in GA4. This involves creating conversion events and adding the tracking code to the relevant pages on your website. Implementing GA4 conversion tracking in a booking platform can be complicated, so that is something you may want to hire a professional to perform. It is beyond the scope of this book.

- **Set Up Custom Dimensions and Metrics.** To track specific data points that are important to your business, such as room types or packages booked for a hotel, you can set up custom dimensions and metrics in GA4.

Once you have implemented GA4 on your hotel website, you can use the GA4 dashboard to analyze your data and gain insights into your website's performance, user behavior, and traffic sources. You can also use the dashboard to set up goals, create reports, and track your progress over time.

Key Metrics

Implementing Google Analytics on your hotel website can provide valuable insights into your website's performance and help you make data-driven decisions about your marketing strategy. Here are some of the key metrics and insights you can learn from Google Analytics:

- **Traffic Sources.** Google Analytics can show you where your website traffic is coming from, such as search engines, social media, or referral sites. By analyzing this data, you can determine which channels are driving the most traffic to your website and adjust your marketing strategy accordingly.

- **Audience Demographics.** Google Analytics can show you the age, gender, and location of your website visitors. This can help you understand your audience and tailor your website content and marketing efforts to better meet their needs.

- **Pageviews.** Google Analytics can show you which pages on your website are getting the most traffic. This can help you identify popular content and optimize your website for user engagement.

- **Bounce Rate.** Bounce rate refers to the percentage of users who leave your website after viewing only one page. By analyzing your bounce rate, you can identify areas of your website that may be causing users to leave and take steps to improve engagement and retention. If your visitors all leave the home page without exploring your site or without converting, then you might have a problem.

- **Conversion Rate.** Conversion rate refers to the percentage of users who take a desired action on your website, such as booking a room or filling out a contact form. By analyzing your conversion rate, you can identify areas of your website that may be hindering conversions and take steps to improve the user experience and increase conversions.

- **Time on Page.** Google Analytics can show you how much time users are spending on each page of your website. This can help you identify areas of your website that may be causing users to leave and take steps to improve engagement and retention.

- **Path Through Site.** Google Analytics will show you the paths your visitors took through your website. This can help you identify problem areas that are causing visitors to drop out, or pathways that are very popular and result in conversions.

- **Site Search.** Google Analytics can show you what users are searching for on your website. This can help you understand user intent and tailor your website content to better meet their needs.

By analyzing these metrics and insights, you can gain a better understanding of how your website is performing and take steps to improve its effectiveness. This may include optimizing your website for search engines, improving user engagement and retention, or tailoring your marketing strategy to better meet the needs of your audience.

Google Tag Manager

Google Tag Manager is a tool that allows you to manage and deploy tracking codes and other marketing tags on your website. It simplifies the process of implementing multiple scripts on your site, and gives you the ability to only fire scripts at certain times, such as on particular page loads or events like button clicks. Here's how you can use Google Tag Manager to implement GA4 on your website:

- **Set Up a Google Tag Manager Account.** To get started, you will need to set up a Google Tag Manager account by visiting **tagmanager.google.com**. This will require creating a Google account if you haven't set one up yet.

- **Create a GA4 Tag in Google Tag Manager.** Once you have set up your Google Tag Manager account, you will need to create a GA4 tag. This involves adding a new tag in Google Tag Manager and selecting the GA4 option.

- **Set Up Triggers.** To determine when the GA4 tag should fire on your website, you will need to set up triggers in Google Tag Manager. Triggers can be based on events, such as pageviews or clicks, or other conditions, such as user location or device type.

- **Add the GA4 Tracking Code to Google Tag Manager.** To begin collecting data, you will need to add the GA4 tracking code to Google Tag Manager. This involves copying and pasting the code snippet provided by Google Analytics into the GA4 tag you created in Google Tag Manager.

- **Publish Your Changes.** Once you have set up your GA4 tag and triggers in Google Tag Manager, you will need to publish your changes to make them live on your website. Don't forget that you need to do this every time you add a new script to Tag Manager!

- **Test Your Implementation.** To ensure that your GA4 implementation is working correctly, you should test it by browsing your website and verifying that data is being collected in Google Analytics.

In addition to implementing GA4, you can also use Google Tag Manager to deploy other marketing tags, such as Facebook Pixel or AdWords Conversion Tracking, on your website. By using Google Tag Manager to manage your tags, you can simplify the process of deploying and managing tracking codes and other marketing tags on your website.

Here is an example of the GA4 tracking code that you would need to paste into your website in order to use Google Tag Manager:

```html
<!-- Google Tag Manager (GA4) -->
<script async src="https://www.googletagmanager.com/gtag/js?id=G-XXXXXXXXXX"></script>
<script>
  window.dataLayer = window.dataLayer || [];
  function gtag(){dataLayer.push(arguments);}
  gtag('js', new Date());

  gtag('config', 'G-XXXXXXXXXX');
</script>
<!-- End Google Tag Manager (GA4) -->
```

The above script would be placed in the header code of every page on your site.

The G-XXX part of the script is your Google Analytics account ID, which you will get from your Google Analytics account. The analytics stuff can be highly complex. There are people who specialize in doing nothing but implementing GA4. If you have trouble setting up GA4, you might want to reach out to a professional experienced in its implementation.

Chapter 10: Marketing by Walking Around

So here we are – the grand finale – where we finally talk about the "marketing by walking around" part. Are you excited?

There is no great mystery here. Marketing by walking around is exactly what it sounds like – you walk around. While you are walking around, you talk to people. You take videos. You take photos. You look for ANYTHING interesting that you can tell your customers and followers and target market about.

Here is an example of how I spend my day at one of my clients' locations:

- I get up in the morning and have breakfast. The hotel clients I work with have great breakfasts, so this is a very easy part of the job! I walk into the breakfast area, phone in hand (I usually leave the camera in the room at breakfast), and snap photos while I get something to eat. I photograph the people working around the kitchen area. I take closeup photos of the food. Not just random photos, either – I stage them to look as attractive as possible. I take photos of the dining area, and the people in it. If there are views from the dining area, I take pictures of those. Then I enjoy breakfast. Right from the start, I am creating material. That is the mindset you need to have – you are CONSTANTLY creating material because you need a LOT of material to work with!

TIP: If you are using an iPhone, you can get some great pictures using the portrait setting, which will apply a nice blur to the background. You can do the same thing by focusing a real camera lens, or with Photoshop, but using the portrait setting on your phone is a quick way to get a professional looking shot with a nice blurred background.

The exception would be if I am working with a restaurant that does not serve breakfast, in which case this process would transfer to lunch or dinner.

I am not just a passive observer of my client's business. I am active. I am involved and immersed in the business. I make myself part of the business. If you are doing this for your own business, then you are already there, which makes the process even easier.

- I return to my room and prepare for the day. I have a backpack with a couple of different camera lenses, extra batteries, water, an umbrella, and various other supplies. I hang my camera around my neck (at the time of this writing, my main camera is a Canon EOS R, a fine mirrorless digital camera that I recommend) and take off.

- Then I hit the streets. I walk around the streets and neighborhoods around my client and take photos and videos of anything going on. Or if I need to go further out, I will get in my car and drive. Wherever there is anything going on or anything interesting to see, that is where I want to go.

- I look to create content from around town as well as outside of town. If there are interesting trails, waterways, waterfalls, mountains, caves or any other noteworthy locations, I will go there and take photos or video.

If your location is not a tourist destination or particularly noteworthy, you may have to look a little harder. But no matter where you are, there are interesting things and notable historic events and figures that you can talk about. So put on your detective hat and find some interesting content.

In the town where I live, there is a gentleman who owns a furniture store that is covered in historical photos from the town's past. He is also very knowledgeable about its history. Find someone like that in your town. Go to him or her, ask questions, take photos. Look for the rich wells of information like that that can help you come up with content.

- I will visit local shops and take photos. Some shops are funny about that kind of thing, so you might want to ask before you just go in and start snapping photos. Some businesses just don't like getting free publicity. Go figure.

- If my client is a hotel, I will visit local restaurants and take photos and notes for writing articles about them. The opposite would apply if my client is a restaurant. Though don't discount the idea of doing some cross-promotion with ANY other local business, even if it is technically a competitor.

- No matter who or what type of business my client is, I am taking photos non-stop while I walk around town. One incredible thing about digital technology is that there is virtually no limit to the amount of multimedia you can create. It's not at all like the "old days" when your camera used film and so you had to be very careful in its use.

Full disclosure: I am not a professional photographer. Taking a really good photo on a real camera is hard. That is one reason I take a TON of photos. The more photos I take, the better my chance of getting some really good ones. I also do use a really good camera. As mentioned, I am using a Canon EOS R mirrorless digital camera. I carry additional lenses around in a camera backpack or in coat pockets so I can get different shots. I will also say that the more photos I take and the more I study the art of photography, the better I get. The same will be for you – the more media you create, the better you will get at it. And definitely take the time to learn how to use your equipment.

- As I go around taking photos, I take them with both my camera and my phone. As mentioned above, getting a good photo from a DSL or mirrorless camera is more difficult. When you do get a good one, it looks amazing. But by also using my phone, I get a whole lot more usable photos that I can use along with the good ones I get from my camera. Plus, sometimes I just get tired of carrying the camera around, so I will leave it behind and just use my phone.

  HOWEVER: I have found having a bigger camera to be an advantage because it is a great talking point. When you walk into a restaurant and sit at a bar with a DSL or mirrorless camera, it attracts attention. It causes conversation, which can lead to you learning interesting tidbits that you can use for content. It's also a relationship starter because people will remember you for the camera. I take it a step further by sometimes attaching a shotgun mic to the top of my camera, which creates the impression that I am a true media professional.

- I always look for elevation. Photos and video taken from an elevated height are always interesting because it's a view you don't see from ground level. Restaurants or other businesses with upper floor balconies are a great option. Get as high as you can. In Gatlinburg, Tennessee, where I often work, there are several spots, such as the Space Needle and Gatlinburg SkyPark, that I can use to get WAY above ground level. Look for anywhere you can get elevated.

- I swap out lenses often. Different camera lenses will give your photos a different look. I use a combination of telephoto, wide angle and various other lenses to mix it up. You are going to need a LOT of material, so photographing the same thing with different lenses gives you more material to work with.

- Sometimes I will do walking around style videos for use with video shorts on platforms like TikTok, YouTube and Instagram. This is a great way to create engaging video content. The short format is all the rage these days.

- I usually eat some time between lunch and dinner. Especially in tourist locations (but really anywhere), it can be time consuming to get a meal at a busy restaurant, so I prefer to eat at odd hours. While I am eating, I will connect my phone to my camera (via a Canon app installed on my phone) and look through the photos taken so far. I will go ahead and download some of the best ones to my phone for convenience. Sometimes in a pinch I will do my social media updates from my phone rather than a computer, so it is very convenient to have good material on my phone.

- I usually sit at the bar if the restaurant has one. I make it a point to try and make connections at local restaurants, shops and hotels. I try to make conversation, and I always tip very well. The same goes for the cleaning staff at the hotel where I am staying. Treat everyone well and be generous. It is just good business. The people who work around town will be more open and willing to help you out if they know you as a generous person.

- I will also talk to and hang around the people who work at my client's location. There are some real characters among those people. Some of them will know the whole story about your business. Some of them will have hilarious stories to tell. You want to know those stories. Some of the best responses I get on social media are when I post photos of the people who work there. One thing you will find is that those photos get many likes on social media from past customers who remember them. The people who work at your business are a rich resource that you need to tap into.

- Although this work is fun, it is tiring. After lunch, I usually return to my room for some rest and time to catch up on some work on my computer. The exception is if I have wound up at a location that is a long drive from where I am staying. Then I will just keep pushing until I have all the media I need for the day.

  Let me reiterate: you need to be taking photos and video non-stop when you are walking by marketing around. You cannot have too much material.

- After some restful work time, I will go back out. I take photos of lit-up city streets, people visiting businesses and bars, bands playing, or anything else that might be going on. Later in the evening, I will sometimes visit a pub and have a couple of beers. But even then, I'm looking for anything of interest to photograph or video. For example, sitting in a restaurant one evening, it began to rain quite hard outside. It created an interesting scene, so I grabbed my camera and snapped some photos through the windows of the rain coming down. I love rain photos because of the shimmer it gives the photos, with rain reflecting the lights of the town on the streets.

  I have made some of my best connections

during those times. When I am in my client's town, I try to embed myself into the local scene as much as possible. You want people around town to know you and like you.

I often have the people I have gotten to know in local bars and restaurants volunteer to show me interesting things on their phones. Unless it is something too personal, I have no problem asking them if I can use it! I tip those guys very well when they help me out like that.

- If there are concerts or other events happening at that time, I will go check those out and take photos and video. It is a good idea to know about what is going on in advance so you can plan for those types of things. If there is a location in town that has performances regularly, that is a well you should mine for material.

- This is a very personal thing. What we are talking about here is the opposite of hiring someone who has never stepped foot in your town to write generic articles based on Google searches or AI. This ain't about a Google search. It is about creating content that is honest and authentic. Your customers and prospects will notice the difference.

- After I spend a few days walking around town generating media and talking to people, I return to my home office and proceed with the task of uploading content every day (at least Monday through Friday). Sometimes I publish a blog post on my client's website and link to that in social media updates. Sometimes I will post something to a YouTube channel and use that. Or it could be a newsletter. Whatever. I create some kind of content every day and feed it through our social media channels. This process doesn't work if you fail to do this with great consistency.

- Most days I will often view my client's Facebook news feed (the news feed of other business Pages we follow) to see if there is anything interesting to share. If I do share something from another Page, I reference it in the post (with an @ followed by their Page name) so that the administrators of the Page become aware that we shared the post.

I have found that is basically impossible to know what piece of content will catch fire. I had a social media post for a client that was a photo that exploded and generated over 1.4 million organic impressions on Facebook. But the thing of it is – it looked very similar to hundreds of other photos I have posted at various times for various clients. But this one caught fire. It would be very expensive to pay for over a million impressions, but we got it for free from this one little photo. That is one reason you post day after day – because you can't predict when something is going to explode or what will explode.

That is also why I create a MASSIVE catalog of photos and video for all of my clients. I never post the same photo twice. I DO reference the same type of post sometimes. For instance, if you are a hotel that serves a great breakfast, then that is something you need to remind your followers of regularly. Post photos of the breakfast you serve, your dining area, the staff and anything that your followers might find interesting.

Getting out and walking around the streets of your town allows you to get to know its secrets – its strange little places that most people don't know about. THAT is where the magic comes from – that original, one-of-a-kind content that gets fed into your marketing system. Stuff that only you have! That's marketing by walking around.

Conclusion

Promoting a hospitality business online is hard work. If you do it the way I recommend, it can also be a lot of fun! There are a lot of pieces that need to fit together.

It starts with research – knowing who your market is, what they look at, what words they use to search for your type of business, etc. That research then gets fed into the website design process.

The website should be well-optimized and fast. Pick a high quality web hosting environment, then build your site around the information uncovered in the research process.

Make sure your site is listed in various directories like Yelp and anything specific to your industry, like Hotels.com.

Next, set up accounts on various social media platforms, starting with Facebook. Then begin posting original content to those platforms, as well as your website, that consists of a mix of various types of content – articles, photos, videos, links to other local businesses, etc. Periodically post an article/blog post and link to that in your social media accounts.

Repeat the content creation/posting process over and over again for the rest of your life.

Create an email newsletter and add a newsletter signup form to your website and social media platforms. Send out an email newsletter once per month or on whatever schedule seems right for your audience.

Get out and start walking around your town. Take a ton of photos and videos. Do this at least once per month, if not more often, then cut up that material into individual pieces.

Some of what we have discussed in this book is techy kind of stuff. For that, you are highly advised to hire somebody who knows what he is doing. Your time is valuable. Don't waste it spinning your wheels.

But the rest of it – you can do.

However…

It still takes a ton of time.

If you could use some help with this, I invite you to contact us at Work Media LLC. We specialize in working with hospitality and would welcome the opportunity to talk to you about how we could help drive traffic and generate more sales for your business.

We'll put on our sneakers and get out and spend the time it takes to create the catalog of content that is required to pull this off. Then we will work our magic using that content to drive traffic and customers to your business.

Look us up at **workmedia.net**.

Now get there and start walkin'!

Resources

WordPress website hosting companies:

- WPEngine.com
- Bluehost.com
- Nexcess.net

Recommended WordPress plugins:

- Autoptimize
- BJ Lazy Load
- WP Fastest Cache
- Yoast SEO
- Divi (WordPress theme)

Keyword research tools

- ads.google.com/aw/keywordplanner/home (must be logged into a Google Ads account)
- SpyFu.com
- Semrush.com

Free images

- Pexels.com
- Pixabay.com
- Unsplash.com
- 123rf.com

Social media platforms

- Facebook.com

- Instagram.com
- YouTube.com
- Pinterest.com
- LinkedIn.com
- TikTok.com

Social Media Management

- Hootsuite.com
- SocialPilot.co
- Buffer.com

Google SEO Tools

- Google.com/analytics
- Search.google.com/search-console
- Business.google.com
- Pagespeed.web.dev

Advertising platforms

- Ads.google.com
- Facebook.com/business
- Business.linkedin.com

Email newsletter platforms

- Mailchimp.com
- GetResponse.com
- ConstantContact.com
- Zapier.com

Citation/review sources

- TripAdvisor.com
- Hotels.com

- Yelp.com
- Travelocity.com

Recommended software

- Adobe Photoshop (for image editing)
- Adobe Dreamweaver (for website editing)
- Adobe Premier Pro (for video editing)
- Topaz Sharpen AI (for fixing blurry photos)

Need Help?

I thank you very much for reading my book! I hope you have found it useful and insightful.

Listen, I live and breathe this stuff. I do it all the time, every day, year-round. I love it. But if you DON'T do it all the time, it can be a real pain. You are very likely busy running your hospitality business. So if you could use some help, I would welcome the opportunity to talk to you.

The way I work is that I (or someone from my company) will spend 2 – 3 days per month at your business and walking around town creating media. Then we spend the rest of the month slicing and dicing that material up into chunks of content for our clients' Internet marketing campaigns. It's time-intensive, but that's why we get results.

Get in touch with us today.

Jerry Work
Work Media LLC
workmedia.net
jwork@workmedia.net
615-745-3094